ORPHEUS

A Poetic Drama

To M.C.B. and A.F. who lovingly produced ORPHEUS
in an unambitious way in Sheffield in 1949.

ORPHEUS

A Poetic Drama
by
OWEN BARFIELD

Edited, with an Afterword by
John C. Ulreich, Jr.

The Lindisfarne Press
1983

Published by The Lindisfarne Press
R.D. 2, West Stockbridge, MA 01266

Cover: Sculpture Statuette of Orpheus and Eurydice
emerging from the Gates of Hell by Auguste Rodin.
By permission of The Metropolitan Museum of Art,
Gift of Thomas F. Ryan, 1910. (10.63.2A)

ISBN: 0-940262-01-0
Library of Congress Catalog Card Number: 82-83247

Printed in the United States of America

Contents

Foreword

The poetic drama which follows was written more than forty years ago. On the occasion of this its belated appearance in print the question arose whether I had better add anything to the extensive commentary material in which it is already embedded, including John Ulreich's Afterword and my own Program Note written for the play's brief and inconspicuous production in 1948. I was at first unwilling to do anything of the sort, because my whole desire and intention in writing it was precisely *not* to express in allegorical, or even symbolical, dress any metaphysical or philosophical speculations or convictions I might then have arrived at, but simply to produce, if I could, a good play; and one moreover which (so far as my pronounced lack of practical Thespian experience allowed) would be "good theater." The convictions and speculations might or might not transpire through the way I dealt with the characters and the plot; they were not to be its object.

Perhaps the personal anecdote of its genesis is relevant here. I had casually mentioned to my friend C.S. Lewis that I seemed to be feeling an impulse to write a play in verse and was wondering about a subject, and at the same time that I wanted to keep clear of the sort of ulterior motives I have just referred to. I recall the occasion very clearly and, though I am not reproducing his exact words, he said in effect: "Why not take one of the myths and simply do your best with it—Orpheus for instance?" To which my mental reaction was, after some reflection: Well, why not? And so, in the event, I got down to it in the limited spare time then at my disposal. Apart from the actual writing, the "getting down to it" consisted almost exclusively of a careful re-reading, with a classical dictionary beside me, of Virgil's presentation of the myth in the fourth *Georgic*. I had "done" it at school, but my recollections of Virgil, apart from a line here or a phrase there, were pitifully vague. I knew of course that there was plenty of literature in existence, based on archaeological and other research, about the figure of Orpheus, the place of Orphism in the history of Greek mythology and philosophy, its influence on early Christianity as evidenced by murals in the catacombs, and so forth; but for the reasons given above I refrained from any attempt to convert my smattering into sound knowledge—an attempt for which I should have had scant leisure in any event. Thus, for example, if Act II Scene ii between Orpheus and the animals should bring into the spectator's or, more likely, the reader's mind St. Paul's remark that the whole creation groaneth awaiting the redemption, or Novalis's aphorism, "Man is the messiah of nature," it will not be because the scene was devised with that intention.

The reluctance I still feel to write anything of a hermeneutic nature is however mitigated in 1982 by the forty-five years' interval since its composition, a gap wide enough to enable me to approach the play almost as if it had been written by someone else. I ask myself therefore, not as its fond parent but as nearly as possible as a judiciously objective observer, whether I can add anything useful; and I think perhaps I can.

It appears to me that, if one is to talk of "themes" and suchlike at all, then there are really *two* themes, or perhaps enigmas, central to the narrative embodied in the drama. Maybe one of them should be labelled "diachronic" and the other "synchronic," though I am not very fond of the words. There is, firstly, "the nature of consciousness" and more particularly the evolution of consciousness in the individual and the race; with, integrally related to that, the theme of sacrificial death and rebirth. And there is, secondly, the theme or enigma of the relation between man and woman. Of these two themes, which are interwoven with one another, the first is dealt with so fully and understandingly by John Ulreich that it would be senseless to try to add anything—except perhaps that, in that context, the symbolism requires not only Orpheus and Aristaeus, as Ulreich points out, but Orpheus, Aristaeus and Eurydice, all three, to be sometimes imagined as a single human entity.

The second theme however seems to me to have a more comparable status, and to fill a more central role than the Afterword may suggest. The play is very much aware (can a play be aware?) of the enigma inherent in the nature of love, of the two antagonisms (again, closely interwoven with one another) experienced there, or the two polarities demanding to be resolved: between flesh and spirit, and between egotism and altruism.

The former makes itself felt particularly in Act I Scene ii, and again in Act IV Scene i, but is present as an undertone throughout; the latter, in Act II Scene ii, culminating, as it does, in Orpheus' resolve to visit the underworld, not in order to cure his own bereavement but to rescue the animals from their natural predicament. But this second conflict—between egotism and altruism—also transpires through minor touches elsewhere, such as the last two stanzas of the Nightingales's song, where Philomela affirms that she sings of her own woe, not out of self-pity but for the sake of her sister Procne (who is not yet aware of the brutal nature of her husband Tereus). Again, the two sub-themes, so to speak, to the theme of love—flesh/spirit and egotism/altruism—coalesce at the crucial moment in Act III Scene i, when Orpheus, expecting to see Persephone but seeing instead, not only Eurydice but Eurydice in the flesh, forgets about the animals and his selfless resolve and is aware only of his reawakened passion.

C.S. Lewis in a Note written in 1948 emphasized, I hope rightly, that *Orpheus* is a mystery drama, not a "problem" one. Yet the scope of its territory is such that it does stretch a sort of tentacle here and there towards issues in the problem class: egalitarianism and its consequences; women's liberation; the permissive society; abortion; the idea of monogamy, its relation to the idea of romantic love, perhaps even the long long history of that relation and that idea; and so forth. Constancy—stead-fastness—loyalty is the crucial stiffener that distinguishes love from passion, as the nuance of aesthetic contemplation is what distinguishes passion from lust; yes, but it is also "the lethargy of custom," repetition, "the same again," and as such is, as the Satyr points out in Act IV Scene i, "the thing they do in Hell." And no wonder, if Coleridge was right to perceive in the lethargy of custom the funeral of imagination and, with that, of all but superficial knowledge. What is the relation between knowing and being? Possibly it is from here, deep down in the mystery of cognition, that the interweaving of the two main themes begins. How, if knowledge without imagination is not knowledge at all, but only a kind of cataloguing? And if knowledge without love cannot be knowledge with imagination?

It is easy to lose one's way among such problems. I like to think that King Minos of Crete attempted, before the mental development of Greece was far enough advanced for it, to tackle the sort of intellectual problems that were later to be handled by

Plato's *Parmenides*, and that, finding it all too much for him, he gave it up and went out and built a labyrinth instead. In the same way the author of *Orpheus* may perhaps be thought of as having "given up" on a tangle of equally bewildering but less abstract problems and gone out and written a play instead. A myth has been defined by someone — German, I believe — as "a symbolic idea with life-renewing force." If one cannot answer questions, or solve enigmas, one can at least write, or rework a myth around them. And since the solid stuff of authentic myth is pretty sure to be wiser than I am, there is always the chance that in my handling of it I may, without knowing it, throw up something that will one day, when the times are riper, help wiser heads than mine to arrive at answers and reach conclusions.

Theme — enigma — question: in its "synchronic" aspect (which is all I am here considering) I am inclined to see *Orpheus* as asking a question. And the question is: can the radiant warmth of erotic affection be expanded or metamorphosed into what the Germans call *allgemeine Menschenliebe*? Can Eros *become* Agape? That Orpheus himself, while still alive, could only half achieve such a transition under the discipline of bereavement, is shown by his reaction to the encounter with his half-regained Eurydice in Hades. The one would have had to cease in order to make room for the other. But of course that is quite literally "not the whole story." I wonder whether the play, taken as a whole, may not be hinting at a transition from, or rather through, Eros to Agape, neither as a Platonic transfer of attention from carnal copy to ghostly original, nor simply as darkness giving way to light, but rather as moonlight brightening imperceptibly into sunshine.

OWEN BARFIELD
South Darenth, Kent
February 1982

A NOTE ON THE PRODUCTION

In Act I Scene i, it is preferable that the actors on the stage, other than **Orpheus** and **Eurydice**, should not actually speak, but should accompany with appropriate gestures and arm-movements the **Choruses** speaking their lines. This is not essential however. But if **Nereus**'s long speech is actually spoken by the actor representing him, it should be accompanied by appropriate movements on the part of the **Nereids**.

The events of Act II Scene i begin a few minutes before the conclusion of those in Act I Scene ii.

The movements of the denizens of Hades at the opening of Act III Scene i should be in the nature of a dance, but jerky and automatic, like badly animated films. Masks may be worn.

The howling of **Cerberus** in this scene should, if possible, emerge from **Hades'** amplified voice in the manner of a defective radio set making noises.

The events of Act IV Scenes i and ii take place simultaneously.

ORPHEUS

A Poetic Drama in Four Acts

CHARACTERS IN THE ORDER OF THEIR APPEARANCE

First Chorus   *A male voice, or voices*

Second Chorus   *A female voice, or voices*

Eurydice   *A* Nereid

Nereus   *A Sea-god, father of* Eurydice *and the other Nereids*

Orpheus   *Son of* Apollo *and the Muse* Calliope

Aristaeus   *Son of* Apollo *and* Cyrene

Charon   *The Ferryman of Souls*

Hades   *The God of the Underworld (the name, as in Homer, also designates his Kingdom)*

Persephone   *His Queen, daughter of* Demeter, *the earth-mother*

Sisyphus   *A wicked soul in torment*

Tantalus   *A wicked soul in torment*

Arethusa   *A nymph, daughter of the river* Peneus, *and sister of* Cyrene

A Satyr

Cyrene   *A nymph, the mother of* Aristaeus

Nereids, Danaïds *(wicked souls in torment)*, Animals, Maenads *(devotees of the wine-god,* Dionysus*)*, River-nymphs, *voices of a* Herald *and of* Ascalaphus *(Hades' spy in the form of an owl)*

Act I Scene i

(Left: Sea. Right: Rocky Shore. Rainbow. Music. **Nereids.** *To them enter more* **Nereids** *dancing, among them* **Eurydice.** *A roll of thunder:)*

First Chorus
  Storm is stopping: stiller grows the sea:
  Now only the arch of Iris' bow
  Tells of the recent wrath of Uranus.
  Old Nereus beneath nodding in his cavern
  Draws into his dream the dropping Calm: 5

Second Chorus
  Creeping from their cover his countless daughters,
  Sporting and splashing in the spume and spray,
  Lie all alive to the lap of waters;
  Laughing they beckon the lazy Calm.

First Chorus
  No man can name them with nice discernment,   10
  Mark one maiden from many others,
  As they thrid through the throng of each other —
  Or grasp their grouping: there grows together
  A knot of Nereids and anon disperses:
  See! two or three: twenty — thirty: 15
  Teasing and tugging at a toy — what is it?

Second Chorus
  Enough! Enough! Nereus rises:

*(***Nereus*** rises from the sea.)*

The Leader of the First Chorus *(for* **Nereus**)
Darling daughters! Dance around me!

Second Chorus
How does it happen that they heed him not?

First Chorus
What are they whispering, one to another?   20

Second Chorus *(dispersedly for some of the* **Nereids**)
To lift its limbs and let them fall,
To see them like seaweed slowly waving
Within the water! Oh, what a game!
A strange starfish! to stroke its rays,
Touch and tickle and twist them about!   25
What a funny fish! What fat fins!
Pale and pink as a pearly shell
And soft as a sponge! What a silly toy!

The Leader of the First Chorus *(for* **Nereus**)
Leave it alone! Let me see it!

First Chorus
Nereus sees now the new plaything,   30
Brine-drenched body, buffeted by the sea,
Of a shipwrecked sailor: severed was its head
By the surge smiting on sharp reefs.
The sea-god starts—sickens strangely.
Huge horror of Heracles,   35
Mazing his memory, is moulding his words.

The Leader of the First Chorus *(for* **Nereus**)
Leave it alone! Let it be!
Never go near it: I know the shape!
Lovely little laughers, now listen to me:—
Slumbering and sleeping on a slope of rock   40
Once I was. One came walking,
Striding over the strand; he was stronger than I.
He had a head: a hard round knob
Sat on his shoulders, like shore on sea.

He lashed me lying asleep on the rock—   45
Me, the master of the moving waves!
Oh the agony, as I awaked
From sleep into self!
I tried to stretch—was strapped helpless!
I struggled to struggle! stock-still!   50
Muscle could not twitch! madness was upon me . . .
Then Metis came, mother of Wit
Wheeling down in a winged shape
With soothing counsel. Sky sent her.
Being checked by force from changing place,   55
She bid me to change my being's self,
Bid Nereus become not-Nereus,
And so escape—instantly hissed
A slippery snake—the snake was Nereus
Held by the body in that hero's fist: 60
A frenzied hound, he frothed and barked . . .
By the neck knuckled and no freer!
Nor fared he better in fish's form:
A dozen creatures he donned in vain
Writhing and wriggling to wrench himself   65
Loose from that grip—
                    Till at last he flamed
Upward in fire—up to Sky's
Wide spaces for wandering in.
Ai! stupid hope! I was still the same!
Ai woe is me! Willy nilly   70
I gave away the guarded secret—
Golden apples in the gardens of the West
By the dragon watched: he drew all forth,
Before he would let me loose from his grip.
Mine was that mystery. Men got it.   75
Icy anguish eats out my heart,
As I tell this tale. Torture wracks me!
Mineral crampings! Movement! Movement!
Measureless motion shall make me better!
Delicate dances to do me delight!   80
In calm choruses, as our custom is,
Dance around me, darling daughters!

*(Dance of the **Nereids** around **Nereus**, in the course of which enter **Orpheus** with his lyre. He stands looking on for a time and then begins to play, taking up the thread of the music. Gradually with his lyre he leads the music at the same time influencing it, so that it becomes less formless and more measured. The character of the dance changes accordingly. As dance and music cease:)*

Orpheus
Do that again! Do that again!

Second Chorus
Startled Nereids stare at the stranger
Stepping forward. Their father frowns: 85
Roar of waters rings out in his word.

The Leader of the First Chorus *(for **Nereus**)*
We shun your shape as shadows the sun:
Will have no hero haunting these our shoals:
Begone quickly from the gods at ease!

Orpheus
Weak as a woman's the weight of my arm,   90
Soft my skin is and shrinks from shock;
No hero am I.

The Leader of the First Chorus *(for **Nereus**)*
        Your head is hard!
I like not your look.

Orpheus
I go at once, if you grant what I ask—

The Leader of the First Chorus *(for **Nereus**)*
Speak then and begone! the shore suits you.   95

Orpheus
The name of the Nereid, whom now I see . . .

The Leader of the First Chorus *(for **Nereus**)*
Enough! No names the Nereids have.

Scene i

Orpheus
    Though she know not her name, a name has she.
    Of all things in earth, and air, and sea
    Zeus guards the names in a golden urn,   100
    A curious casket.

The Leader of the First Chorus (*for* **Nereus**)
          And keeps the key.

Orpheus
    One key of his grace gave he the Muses,
    Memory's daughters. My mother was one.
    When most my song soars in splendour,
    When ether blossoms in bursts of sound,   105
    Like a butterfly born on its tremblings
    Flits my mother, a messenger from Zeus —
    Hovers over my head with heavenly wings:
    They brush my lips: Love engenders:
    The tip of my tongue tastes a name   110
    Unuttered before by any mouth,
    Fresh and dewy from the depths of the urn.

The Leader of the First Chorus (*for* **Nereus**)
    What a whirr of words! You weary me.

Orpheus
    Her name: tell me!

The Leader of the First Chorus (*for* **Nereus**)
          I know it not.
    Now get you gone: graceless asker!   115

Orpheus (*to the* **Nereids**:)
    Dancers, dance me that dance again!

Second Chorus (*confusedly, for* **Nereids'** *mocking*)
    "Dancers-dances-that-dance's-game!"

Orpheus
    Again, I said, I said again.

Second Chorus (*as before*)
> Again, he said, he said again!
> Ha ha ha ha ha ha!   120
> What whirring words. Wonderful creature!
> Again! ha ha ha ha!
> Jabber and jargon and jibberish!
> What land-language! To listen and laugh!

Orpheus
> Mother of my mother—might you but help me.   125
> Meaning's mystery I would make them feel!
> Listen, ladies, you laugh at "again"
> As a silly sound. Say if you never
> Heard sweet echo over the sea
> Answer back to the angry roarers   130
> An angry roar?
> Mock and mimic the mewing of gulls
> With mewing of gulls? Your mouths mocked me
> But a moment back: they mimicked my mouth.
> Will you play but a game to please me now?   135
> Pretend you be Echo—an easy task.
> What Echo would do I'll do with my lyre:
> Do with your dancing what Echo would do!

The Leader of the First Chorus (*for* **Nereus**)
> Laughers, leave him! I like not this game.

> (**Orpheus** *begins to play the same music, the* **Nereids** *to dance the same dance as before. When dance and music are at their height, suddenly* **Orpheus** *breaks off. Dance and music cease.*)

Orpheus
> Eur-yd-i-ce!   140

The Leader of the First Chorus (*for* **Nereus**)
> Listen not! Listen not! Leave him! Come!
> Answer not, Nereid! Or all is lost!
> Thetis was named; the thief Peleus
> Who bound her down—she bore him a son
> (When the name is come, the Nereid goes).   145

Second Chorus *(for the other* **Nereids***)*
Listen not! Listen not! Leave him! Oh come!
Not to answer him! Nereid! Sister!

Eurydice
Not to answer him — Orpheus — I . . .

(**Orpheus** *turns and begins to walk away.*)

Second Chorus
Not to follow him! Nereid! Nereid!

(**Orpheus** *walks slowly off without looking back,* **Eurydice**
following behind.)

Second Chorus
Not to follow! Oh, Nereid! Turn!   150

— Curtain —

Scene ii

(Scene: A grassy slope with a tree growing on it and at some distance from the tree a thicket of rose bushes forming a kind of arbour entered by a natural arch. In the distance, on the one side, mountains; on the other, the sea.)

(The curtain rises discovering **Orpheus** *and* **Eurydice** *seated.)*

Eurydice
Orpheus! Love! She grows bewildered:
It was otherwise at first
When you led her from the water—

Orpheus
Was it sweeter in the water?

Eurydice
And she followed where you led,   5
High upon this moveless ocean
Of the trees and the mountains,
Where the mountains never fall
And the valleys never rise—
Over brown earth, over green earth—   10

Orpheus
Was it better on the brown earth?

Eurydice
It was otherwise. Even after,
When she dared to overtake you
And they wandered hand in hand,
Orpheus with Eurydice,   15

Looking through their twice two eyes
Out upon this frozen ocean
And were pleased with what they saw.

Orpheus
Was Eurydice more happy?

Eurydice
She seemed otherwise—
                    Oh Orpheus!   20
Now it is *you* who follow
Where she leads—your eyes that follow
Or, when I repose, they rest
Even as now, like the moonlight
Falling blank upon the water,   25
On my face and on my breast.

Orpheus
Does its falling—do they hurt you?

Eurydice
Dear, the white hands of my father
Laid on my bowed head in blessing
Rested not more lightly—yet—

Orpheus
                  Yet?   30

Eurydice
Yet I know not. Listen . . . Look!
(She takes up a handful of earth.)
Earth will crumble, but earth will not
Vanish away between my fingers
Leaving nothing—like sand.
When I do the thing with sand,   35
If I rub my hands together,
When I shake them, they are clean.
Poor Eurydice's soiled fingers!
Who shall lave them?

Orpheus *(taking her hand and kissing it)*
Lips of Orpheus!

Eurydice
Lips that summoned and she followed!   40
Lips that sang! loved lips! Oh, Orpheus!
You have changed! I remember,
I remember how your singing
Once unfroze this silent ocean
And unlocked the lakes of land   45
And unlocked the shapes of things:
Once you sang of all I gazed on
Till its self was your singing,
Till the mountains sank to valleys,
And the valleys rose to mountains   50
And the sky and earth and air
Floated all together, ringing,
Speaking with the tongue of Orpheus.
    You have changed! Now bare
Is the earth, the sky is silent   55
Emptied of the voice of Orpheus,
Emptied of the life of Orpheus,
Robbed of their great gift of Orpheus.
When I see them, I see nothing.
All his songs are now of one—   60
One—Nereid—and she—

Orpheus
                      Chides him!
Other sages chide their pupils
For neglect to learn the lesson,
But Eurydice the tyrant
Scolds them when they learn too well!   65
She is "otherwise"!
                      Eurydice,
Praise me not for voicing nature!
When the Whole speaks through me,
I am not. The languid urchin
Vibrates to the moon-thrilled sea   70

But, abiding not, is nothing.
He who says: Lo, what I gaze on
Is the same as even now,
He abides and knows and loves it,
Clinging: steadfastness is all.   75
Once you sighed: What is a lover?
From yourself I learnt the answer:
Seeing less, he sees more clearly,
Knowing less he knows more nearly,
Steadfastness is all. Unending   80
Is the might of constancy.
Through the part, the little wicket,
Shines the glory, burns the Whole,
And Orpheus, finding new earth, air and sea,
Still hymns them all, hymning Eurydice!   85

Eurydice
What? I fear you! like a stranger's
Beat your words upon my shore!

Orpheus
Like a stranger's! Oh most cruel!
This, the very thread that bound us!
Nay, but you *shall* understand!   90
Help me, now, Mnemosyne!
    Listen: many many days
Orpheus lingered with his lyre
Watching, charmed, the Nereids dancing
Over silver-sanded bays: 95
They were as the waves to him,
Melting one into the other
In the laughter of their glancing
And indifference of their ways,
Till—as sleepers grow uneasy,   100
Unaware that they are waking,
As the dawn creeps colder—
He was slowly disenchanted.
Nereid passed with flashing hair:
Orpheus saw that she was fair,   105

But he only thought: — "not *that* one!"
Till I shouted: "She is *there*,
She herself!" . . . till the day
When my mother gave me strength
Greater than your mighty father's —   110
When she touched my trembling lips
And they opened like a flower
On your name: Eurydice!
Oh Eurydice, this power
Even now is moving me   115
When you think me like a stranger,
When you start, as from danger!

Eurydice

Oh cease not! Your word is magic!
Orpheus! Master! At my feet?
Say, was this — this your meaning   120
When you spoke of "constancy"?

Orpheus

Even the same.

Eurydice

        Oh, lovely thing!
Yet I fear — oh man, I fear!
Travellers love the journey better
Than the goal they travel to.   125
Having mastered once my name,
Will you weary of the same?
The same Eurydice year after year?
Why do I speak in this strange way?
I fear!

Orpheus (*takes his lyre and plays*)
        Hear you?   130
(*He plays again, this time pointedly repeating one of the
phrases over and over again.*)

Heard you? Heard you? Which was sweeter?
Did you weary of "the same"?
Sweetness is song's life-blood. Then blame not me,
If my sweet songs are all—Eurydice!

Eurydice
    Oh my lover! I am nothing! 135
    I will chide no more! Yet—Orpheus—
    If't be true, as you persuade me,
    You have found a deeper beauty—
    Oh, how can I not be jealous?
    I who never see this beauty, 140
    I who may not share it with you,
    As we shared in the beginning,
    When we sacrificed together?
    Orpheus' singing gave me eyes,
    Eyes to see the world he sang of. 145
    Now he sings of what he gave me.
    So the gift is all in vain:
    Eyes may never see themselves!

Orpheus
    Fairest, in our cup of pleasure
    Is this drop the only pain? 150
    Had I means to melt it wholly—
    Tell me, what would follow then?

Eurydice
    I know not—I may not tell you.

Orpheus
    I *have* means. Hephaestus lately
    Made for golden Aphrodite 155
    By her own command this—

Eurydice
                Oh!

Orpheus

    What? Alas, what see you? Show me!
    Where? Where?

Eurydice

               The tree-bole moved!
    There! the root—the lichen-spotted—

(A serpent rears its head from the foot of the tree.)

Orpheus

    Hush! Be stone! 'Tis death to hasten!   160
    Hush! Oh lyre of Orpheus, help us!
    Save us with your mystery!

*(**Orpheus** plays over the same melody as before. He repeats the melody, this time repeating the phrase in it. The third time, the phrase is repeated three times, and so on, until at last he is playing the one phrase over and over again. The serpent sleeps.)*

    Charmed! Asleep! Strange! I knew
    I had power to bind with music
    Other beasts, but not the Serpent—   165
    Now my music, strong and new,
    Lulls him too, lulls him too!

Eurydice

    Come away—elsewhere! I fear!

Orpheus

    No. It sleeps. It sleeps enchanted!
    Gongs and trumpets would not rouse it.   170
    Nothing now can penetrate its
    Stillness save a treading heel.
    Stir we not!
               Hephaestus lately
    Made for golden Aphrodite
    By her own command this engine,   175

Scene ii

Which my musical fingers copied
Deftly for my darling!
(He gives her a mirror.)
Take it!

*(The light dims slightly. **Eurydice** shudders. She raises the mirror and looks into it.)*

What say you?

Eurydice *(slowly)*
I have business with this lady in the bower. Anon
I will return.

Orpheus
Leave me your scarf, while you are gone! 180

*(**Eurydice** unbinds her scarf and throws it to him, as she disappears into the arbour. **Orpheus** raises the scarf to his lips and buries his face in it.)*

Second Chorus
But who is this approaching?

First Chorus
Firm of tread,
His gait and gear are like a countryman's.

Second Chorus
His sunny curls reveal Apollo's child.

First Chorus
His confident heel is weighty on the ground.

Second Chorus
Look in his eyes!

First Chorus *(after a brief pause)*
I have seen —

Second Chorus

Be still! Be still!   185

And watch what time and action shall fulfill!

(**Aristaeus** *enters, wearing thick gloves and carrying nets.*)

Aristaeus
Quick! Have they come this way?

Orpheus

This way?

Aristaeus

The swarm!

Orpheus
The swarm?

Aristaeus

Ye gods! Wake up! I am following my
swarm—

(Looking up into the tree:)
A swarm of bees! Wake up, man! Are they here?

Orpheus
I am awake. I neither saw nor heard them.   190

Aristaeus
Ah, then they must have veered some other way.
(He begins to go.)

Orpheus
Unless they passed without my noticing!

Aristaeus *(stopping and looking)*
What in the world could be more noticeable!

Orpheus
Unless a man's own thoughts were swarming—

Scene ii

Aristaeus

Swarming?

Orpheus
Ye gods! Wake up! Swarming around their Queen!   195

Aristaeus
Their Queen?

Orpheus
O you know nothing of the heart!
Farewell! Follow your swarm and fill your hive!

Aristaeus (*dropping his nets, approaching nearer to* **Orpheus**
and looking him up and down)
I know your carping kind—wind-swollen stripling—

Orpheus
I was too brusque. I crave your pardon, Sir—

Aristaeus
Who think, because we yeomen go about   200
Without a zither slung about our shoulders,
We are outcast from harmony—have no hearts
Because we do not wear them on our sleeves—

Orpheus
I said not so.

Aristaeus
You looked it.

Orpheus
And repented!
Will you not tell me—

Aristaeus
Listen! A month ago   205
My only son, Actaeon, saw the Goddess
Enter the bath; and, for this accident,
She—set her dogs on him. And he, my son,
Was torn to pieces and devoured by them.

Orpheus *(horror-struck)*
    Zeus! and you still can spare a thought for bees!   210

Aristaeus *(sternly)*
    Earth stands not still, because a farmer longs
To die—the goats want milking just the same.

Orpheus
    Yet grief—

Aristaeus
        Hateful exertion physics grief.

Orpheus
    Grief, unresolved in music, is a wolf,
A starving wolf that hollows out the soul—   215

Aristaeus
    Silence! . . . Besides, when all goes prosperously,
The gentle hum, intense, of fanning plumes
About the brood is harmony enough,
Thrilling, and filling with warmth the hollow skep,
Even as my Father's lute-strings fill the sky—   220
Father Apollo!

Orpheus
        Apollo! "Father Apollo!"
What, are we brothers?

Aristaeus
        Aristaeus I!
My mother is the river-nymph, Cyrene.

Scene ii

Orpheus
My mother is the Muse, Calliope,
Who named me Orpheus.

Aristaeus
                       I must find my bees!   225
Thereafter we will talk.

Orpheus
                   I shall be near.

(**Aristaeus** *goes offstage.*)

Orpheus (*starting*)
The serpent! Ha, how comes it I forgot
To warn my brother! And he passed so near!
I will despatch it now.
(*He moves towards the tree.*)

(**Eurydice** *appears in the entrance to the arbour, richly
adorned, and with her flowing hair bound up in the fashion of
a Greek lady.*)

Eurydice
Come!

(**Orpheus** *turns at the sound of her voice, hesitates a
moment, looking back at the tree, then follows her. Faint
music.*)

Aristaeus (*re-entering near to the spot where he left his nets:*)
           Dolt, to forget the gear!   230
(*He picks up his nets, then looks up and round:*)
Where is my brother gone?
(*The music swells a little louder.*)
                  What is this place?
(*He looks fixedly at the arbour, as the music again increases
slightly in volume, though it is still not loud. Musingly:*)
Harmony!
(*He sits dejectedly:*)
          O let be! What use? What use?

The Voice of Orpheus *(from within the bower; distant and dreamy)*
    This is this moment! Seize it! Seize it! Trap the Fates!
    The dragon sleeps. The dragon sleeps. Wide stand the
                    gates.

Aristaeus *(still thinking of his son)*
    To walk with the eyes shut were to go blind,   235
    To walk with the eyes open was to look,
    To see ambrosial flesh was to desire,
    To lust was to pursue—all innocent!

The Voice of Orpheus *(as before)*
    I am among the golden apples of the West.

The Voice of Eurydice *(from within the bower; distant and dreamy)*
    Lo, where my golden apples round thy cheeks are
                    pressed.   240

Aristaeus
    Little Actaeon! Artemis and her hags,
    Her barren hags, to uphold chastity
    By murdering—Actaeon!—that soft throat
    And all the snarling fangs! No! No! No! No!
    His tender nape, where, when he was a baby,   245
    His hair came down into a twisted point!
    Actaeon! Gods! My Son—never again!

The Voice of Eurydice *(as before)*
    The thirsty earth drinks deep cool draughts of blessed
                    rain

The Voice of Orpheus *(as before)*
    And thanks the Sun with blossoms open wide—Again!

Aristaeus
    The air is strange here. It revives my strength.   250

Scene ii

The Voice of Orpheus *(as before)*
Make me immortal! Condescend! Thy votary lift!

Aristaeus
The breeze is full of laughters, little ones,
Like little roguish boys that sparkle round
Ripe mouths and breasts and necks, to keep us kissing!

The Voice of Eurydice *(as before)*
Thus Aphrodite thanks Hephaestus for his gift!   255

The Voice of Orpheus *(as before)*
Yea! yea! Where now is Orpheus?

The Voice of Eurydice *(as before)*
                         Where Eurydice?

The Voice of Orpheus *(as before)*
The weary land turns home at last and slips into the sea!

Aristaeus
I feel them on my cheek. I see them not.
When have I felt them so before? Ho! *Pan!*
Pan! It is thou! I know thou art near this place!   260
Yea, I hear all thy whispered promises:
I to be glad again — Yea, I accept.
Where art thou? Hush! I hear them now — voices!

Orpheus *(as before)*
Eurydice! delicious! Orpheus gropes forlorn! Whither?

Eurydice *(entering from the bower, looking back)*
I go to fetch the joy of my return!   265

Aristaeus
The quickening breeze blows through my hair: my
                        blood,
Spurning black humours, leaps in longings warm:
Old summers rustle through my memory —

(*seeing* **Eurydice***)*
A nymph!
(*He chuckles:*)
      O Pan, this was most like thyself!
Dear god of opportunity! Lady!   270

Eurydice
What is this? What are you?

Aristaeus

          Lady!

Eurydice

            My Lord!
(*Aside:*)
So alike, and so unlike!

Aristaeus

        Comfort and joy!
(*He places his arm round her.*)

Eurydice (*bewildered*)
Master?

Aristaeus

      Sweet mistress! Wilt thou have it so?
Come! we will go together!

Eurydice (*breaking away from him:*)
           O no! no!

Aristaeus
Cold? Then by force!

Eurydice
       Oh!
(*He rushes at her.* **Eurydice** *shrieks and runs from him,
passing the tree:*)
      The serpent! I am stung!   275

Scene ii

(She falls to the ground.)

Aristaeus *(kneeling and embracing her:)*
 One kiss, O nymph, one kiss! Still fragrant is thy
              breath!
 Still warm thy dazzling bosom!

Eurydice
          Ah, how cold is death!
 (She dies.)

Aristaeus
 Clay in my arms! O empty hell! So Pan keeps faith!
 (He rushes offstage.)

Orpheus *(offstage, louder than before)*
 My arms are too long empty! Where art thou, my life?

Second Chorus *(for the Soul of **Eurydice**)*
 The great deep rises round. I cannot see my father! 280
 I sink! My husband! O great rock, be firm for me!

Orpheus *(entering from the arbour and looking about him but
 without seeing **Eurydice***:)*
 What, no reply! Aha! my roguish lady wife!
 Orpheus is coming: soon upon his widowed cheek
 You shall pay heavy forfeit for this game of hide and
         seek!

     —Curtain—

Act II Scene i

(The River Styx. **Eurydice** *with* **Charon** *in a boat in front of
a curtain concealing the back part of the stage.)*

Eurydice
I sink! My husband! Oh great rock! be firm for me!

Charon
Well, I like that! I've worked this ghastly boat
For ever since the Titans crashed: afloat
Both day and night—if you're not satisfied,
You can ghastly well stay on the other side!   5
 Don't you be anxious, Lady, in this gloom—
Safe as a coffin in a ghastly tomb
And caulked as tight she is. Feel better? There!
I could see you was plucked. The change of air
Makes some of 'em turn green a bit—

Eurydice
                                    Why does he glare?   10

Charon
Sometimes they shivers and sometimes they whines—
You're not like that—Let's see your burial lines!
Properly stamped, I hope, and duly marked?
Should have produced 'em before you embarked.
Come on, let's see it!
(Aside:)   Doesn't seem to hear!   15
Or do you want to spend a hundred year
Wandering up and down the wrong side, Miss?
Speak up! Here, this won't do! I can't have this.
What d' you suppose the rule's intended for?
Oh very well, then, back we go to shore!   20

(Makes a show of putting the boat about.)

Eurydice

    What a whirr of words!

Charon

    What's that? Oh well—for once—I don't like breaking
    The rules: you'll give a written undertaking
    For proper burial? Will you?
    (Aside:)   She means yes.
    As I was saying, it's a heavy boat   25
    To take across. I only get the groat
    One way! Not much to get a drop to keep
    The cold—My ghastly eyes, the ghost's asleep!
        Ahem! . . . Ahem!
    (He bangs the gunwale with an oar and then shakes her more and
    more roughly, but with no effect.)
    Come on, wake up! You can't die here, you know!   30
    Wake up! Wake up! Hoy ho! Hoy ho! Hoy ho!
    (Gives it up.)
    Here, what's all this? What am I 'sposed to do?
    I think I'll leave this job, I really do.
    Nothing goes right and proper—it's a sin—
    Ever since that great hero butted in . . .   35
    Stands on the bank, still living if you please:
    "Charon? Oh, Charon, I am Heracles:
    Take me across at once!" I says: "I can't,
    You're breathing!" Then he answers: "No, I aren't."
    "Liar," I says, "you are, you know you are!   40
    You don't catch me acting irregular!"
    "Oh well," he says, "suppose I am! What now?"
    "Aha," I says, "produce your golden bough!"
    That dishes him. You could see he was riled,
    But more surprised like—like a ghastly child.   45
    "Take me across!" he says. I says: "I won't!"
    "Take me across!" he says. Cripes, if he don't
    Stamp like a tyrant—fairly lets it rip!
    "Look here," I says, "old son, none of your lip!

Didn't you hear me say just now you can't   50
Without a golden—" "Golden bough my aunt!"
He yells. Before I knew what he had done,
He'd jumped into the boat and sowsed me one
That knocked me silly; next across the stream
He forced her like a darting quinquereme,   55
Straining her planks . . . gets treated like a god!
And, when he's gone, *I* get a year in quod!
(The boat has now reached the farther shore.)
Oy! Here we are, aground!
(Standing up and raising his left arm in salute:)
                                    Hail, Hades!

*(The curtains part, disclosing, brightly lit, the centre part only of
the stage. Two thrones side by side, on one of which Persephone
is seated, while* **Hades***, who has risen from the other, advances
down stage towards the boat.)*

Charon *(again raising his left arm in salute:)*
    Hail, Hades! Charon with one soul on board
    Reports delivery and salutes his Lord.   60

Hades
    What name?

Charon
                    I don't know, Sir, I've done my best.
    I can't get nothing out of this deceased.
    It's all one with the way things happen now, Sir,
    Since that man crossed without a golden bough, Sir.
    I would have stopped him: No, I says, I *won't*.   65
    Take me across! he says. Hanged if he don't
    Stamp like a tyrant—"Golden bough my aunt!"
    He yells. Before I knew what—

Hades
                            Yes, we can't
    Go into all that now. Is she interred?

Charon
He'd jumped into the boat and knocked —

Hades

You heard!   70

Charon
Yes. That is, No. Well — not to say *interred*
She isn't. But I understand she's making
Arrangements.

Hades
Did you get her undertaking?

*(**Charon** nods.)*

Written?

Charon
Yes, written, yes.

Hades

The usual file —
That's all I want.

Charon *(saluting:)*
Farewell, Hades, and Hail!   75
Charon returns —

Hades
You fool, you haven't thought —
Tell Rhadamanthus to prepare the Court.

Charon
I'll go at once.
*(Exit **Charon** towards Hell.)*

Persephone *(who has risen and come forward to join **Hades**:)*
Oh, that uncouth old man!

Poor shrinking ghosts! Why, why do you insult them
With such a shocking welcome? This was my task!   80
I would take them by the hand and lead them gently
And by such soft gradations of approach
As Hesperus ushers daylight towards the dark.
Out of deep sweet fresh sleep they should awake
To find that they were dead. Oh, I would be   85
As tender as a shepherd with his sheep.

Hades

Persephone, why does she come asleep?

Persephone

She is born of the waves, wherein the world
Swims helpless still. She can see nothing here.
It is all so hard and small and close at hand.   90
I know her well.
She is a Nereid of the sunlit sea.
I have seen her dancing with her dancing sisters
On the bright Aegean's wind-broken floor.
She is a Nereid of the moon-thrilled sea.   95
She will follow me sleeping, as the flood
Follows the wandering moon. Come, Nereid, come!
(She helps **Eurydice**, *who moves like a somnambulist, up on to
the stage.*)

Hades

What's that you say? She is of Nereus' kind?
No reason for indulgence to my mind
Or weak concession. No. Quite the reverse.   100
A cause for special caution and a curse.
The fountain Arethusa late I found
Prying and poking past us underground,
Gurgling a crumbling way through limestone rocks,
And running round old granite with lax locks.   105
Officious nymph, of whom I took no heed.
Yes, and what followed after she was freed?
The moment she poured out into the air,
She ran and told your Mother where you were!

Persephone
> Alas, poor Hades—and poor Demeter!   110

Hades
> Who robs me of my Queen for half each year!

Persephone
> Gentle, to need me so!
> (To **Eurydice**:)   Come, Lady, come!
> I will conduct you to Elysium!

Hades
> Stop! Will you stop! After I've just explained!
> She must be cross-examined, judged, and chained.   115

Persephone
> No! You forget your oath. You may not touch
> With your infernal chains a sleeping soul.
> When I became, from a reluctant thrall,
> The not unwilling queen of all your dead,
> It was upon these terms. You are not free   120
> To fetter any souls which are not free!

Hades
> Good! That was good, my love! But now—let's see:—
> To seek to bind me by a rule I made
> Implies a rule that rules must be obeyed,
> Therefore, if chains must wait, the usual test   125
> By the same token must be closely pressed:
> The usual test when my good Minos makes,
> The subject (I have often noticed) wakes!

Persephone
> Others perhaps—not she! She is not the same.
> The questions and the probings and the noise   130
> And all your pin-pricks will but make her sleep
> Sounder than ever.

Hades
We can only try!
(Drives a needle into the thigh of **Eurydice**, *who does not move.)*
Why, this is really extraordinary!
Nereid, you say? Or nymph or naiad? Well,
We shall make something of her yet in Hell.   135
Though how she, an immortal, came to die
Is what you love so much—a mystery!

Persephone
Dear vulgar God! Will you not leave it so?
You see you cannot choose but let her sleep.
(She assists **Eurydice** *to lie down.)*
We know not what the living are about   140
Since Heracles—

Hades
Will you please leave that out!

Persephone
Then, when she wakens, I shall take her hand
And lead her gently to Elysium.

*(During the ensuing lines Hades and Persephone retire together
to the throne, on which they seat themselves.)*

Hades
She will not wake. How can she? What should wake
   her?

Persephone
Say—something still unknown to you and me.   145

Hades
In that same instant, then, she shall be chained!

Persephone
No! I shall lead her to Elysium.

Hades

How do you know she will agree to go?

Persephone

Why, what should cause her to wish otherwise?

Hades

Say—something still unknown to you and me!   150
Aha!
To introduce the concept 'unknown cause'
Is in discourse the most extreme of flaws.
If we infer what *must* be from what *might*,
Then each effect implies its opposite,   155
Which is absurd.

Persephone

          Oh, you are wonderful!
I love to feel you thinking with such fire
Of nothing!

Hades

        Hm! Not *when*, but *if* she wake,
She will be chained at once—make no mistake.

Persephone

Inexorably fixed in your resolve   160
As you are famed to be! Then, if you cross me,
How shall I murmur at the thing I love?
But tell me this. Tell me, why do you strive
To bar the entrance to Elysium?

Hades

There is a plant which prospers far too well   165
In that mild air—Disloyalty to Hell!
Above they call it "Goodness." Underground
We strip away that high falutin' sound
And call it—faugh! the thing's a poison tree—
The very core of *all* disloyalty—   170
The rest can Hell, in systematic course,

Or by persuasion straighten or by force:
Here the right treatment for each soul, soon found,
Turns the lone eagle to the social hound:
We force some souls, like parrots, to recite   175
And learn by repetition to think right;
Others from lectures learn that they pursued
Even in selflessness a private good!
Misers who lend, still hoard, their vested pelf;
Selflessness, as an act, posits a self,   180
And that's the seat of conscience, treason, rot,
The running sore, the itch, the leprous spot,
The nasty pimple from the plague of life
That swells, with death in contumacious strife.
Who strives to become better, strives to excel: 185
All must be equal, all be one, in Hell.
And rightly to be one is, not to be,
To cease out of existence into me!
I am the self denied, the breathed-out breath,
I am the One, I am the All, for I am Death!   190

(After a few moments' silence, an owl hoots.)

Persephone
I hear Ascalaphus!

Hades
                    My best of spies!
Ascalaphus, than whom no spy in Hell
Ever sneaked better, or sneaked half so well!
You changed him to an Owl! 'Twas through his eyes
I pierced the dangerous ferment of that Scum   195
Of Hell—the spirits in Elysium!
Their stubborn stand against our corporate death
Amazed me: I enquired what lay beneath,
And learned from him the truth—the Blest up there
Somehow keep contact with the Upper Air!   200

Persephone

    True, but you stopped it: all the ways you closed.
    Guarded the passes—even the earthquake faults
    Are crammed with loads of boulders. Where is the
                  danger?

Hades

    It is not stopped. There's something passes still.
    I cannot check it, tighten how I will.   205
    I need the eyes of Argus. Rumours tell
    That *bees* crawl down through crannies into Hell:
    Fat, winged bees out of bright sunlight come
    Visiting blossoms in Elysium.

Persephone

    Or do they carry back into the light   210
    Some precious essence of the virtuous dead?

Hades

    Equally undesirable, my love!

Persephone

    Why does this intercourse vex you so much?
    When summer carpets the earth-crust with flowers
    And all the upper air bursts into life   215
    Humming and whelming, as warm floods of sleep
    Sing round the prone limbs of a weary man,
    I pass above and walk among the flowers
    Beside my Mother. When the dark returns
    And the black frost sparkles the vigilant air,   220
    I too return below to be your Queen
    And hold intense discourse with your sharp wit.
    I also am a traveller to and fro:
    Have I done any harm by being so?

Hades

    You are Persephone. You trace your birth   225
    Back to Demeter, Mother of the Earth,
    But she—

(indicating **Eurydice***:)*
> I do not trust these water beings!

Persephone
What do you fear?

Hades
>   I will not let my act
Facilitate some vague subversive pact—
The little leak that ends a cataract!   230
"Pact" did I say? The word should have been "brew."
Contact amounts to mixture with that crew!

Persephone
Pact between *whom*?
(Raising her arm in salute:)
>   Hail paramount Hades!
Lord of the Styx and frightened of the bees!

Hades
If bees were always bees and nothing more,   235
Your last remark, I grant, would be a score.
Ascalaphus—before you spoilt his eyes—
Once spotted Proteus through that same disguise,
Proteus, of whom we nothing (to be strict)
Can even predicate, much less predict,   240
The formless, watery god—the life of Light
Undarkened into form! O, once those bright
And beauteous beings mingle with the Blest:—

Herald *(offstage)*
Oyez! Oyez!
Hades, Lord of Cocytus, Acheron,   245
Avernus, Lethe, Styx and Phlegethon:

*(***Hades*** rises to his feet, as the Herald utters his name, and during the rest of the speech comes forward to where* **Eurydice** *is
lying.)*

Whereas a deceased person (name unknown)
Is charged forthwith to appear before the throne
Of Rhadamanthus, and whereas Charon
By affidavit duly sworn hath shown   250
Said corpse to have been cremated blood and bone,
Said ashes sealed within an urn of stone
With customary rites all duly done—
Now then the Infernal Lords conciliar
Summon said soul to answer at the bar!   255

Persephone
I still believe that I shall have my way!

Hades (*pulling the sleeping* **Eurydice** *roughly to her feet:*)
The rules must be observed. She may not stay.
Now, royal advocate, will you escort
This non-committal client to the Court?
She may need the assistance of an arm.   260

Persephone (*rising and coming forward:*)
I will. Your judges cannot work her harm.
(*She takes* **Eurydice** *by the hand and guides her out still
sleeping.*)

Herald (*offstage*)
Oyez! Oyez!

(**Hades** *turns and faces the exit, draws himself up and raises
his arm in salute.*)

Herald
Hades, God of Cocytus, Acheron,
Avernus, Lethe, Styx and Phlegethon . . .

— *Curtain* —

Scene ii

(Darkness. **Orpheus** *is seated beside a glowing fire, alone.)*

Orpheus
  Dark!
  The very sun is dark!
  How shall I go on breathing here in space
  Dark with the vanished brightness of her face?
  (Sings:)
      Eurydice! Eurydice!   5
  Smooth-gliding nymph, bright wife,
  Who floated down the river of my life
  Sleeping and waking by my side,
  Clothed in her beauty's seamless vesture
  And slipping liquid without pause   10
  From gesture into lovely gesture!
  Lovely in motion, beautiful in rest,
  She filled with light the light
  But filled more full the night,
  When all my round horizon was her breast.   15
  Come back, oh Queen, oh bride,
  Whose kisses are my only laws!
  Hateful my heavenly birth!
  Flesh—of my flesh the monarch and the thrall—
  Be in my veins my life, my blood, my all!   20
  Again
  Be thou possessed!
      Thine arms about me placed
  Melt me in streaming ocean: mine around thee pressed
  Draw down my music spirit to the earth,   25
  To be the girdle round thy waist,
  And lo!

My mother and the Muses and their train
Troop from above below
And are enchanted in the solid sphere   30
And caught down here!

Hush! Said I so?
This dreaming with the streaming blood
Leads me on, and leads me to no good.
Back! Orpheus! Back! for fear.   35
Oh traitor bard! Oh sacrilegious Son!
What! like some gross ox trampling holy ground!
I will be steadfast in my misery.
    I see her gazing as she used—oh, song!
Out of my misery   40
Pass thou into a strain more high and strong,
Where thou shalt of Eurydice be found
Worthy in sense and sound:
(Sings:)
Sing me, oh Muse, how once I groped for hours
    Brooding in anguish on my coming years   45
When, like white dew that falls on purple flowers,
    A silence fell athwart my storm of tears:
The iron band across my breast was broken
    And for a time such grief was its own balm:
It was evening; "Orpheus!" my name was spoken,   50
    "Lift up thine eyes and in the blue find calm!"
I gazed intense and rose into wide ringing
    Fields of bright ether where Apollo sings
And saw the solid earth beneath me swinging
    Soft in the shadow of the spirit's wings . . .   55

        Her soaring ended,
           My soul descended
        With folded wings
           In humbler wise.

        Oh, lovely Creature!   60
           Oh holy Nature!
        Now first I saw thee
           With open eyes!

One came to meet me
    And soft did greet me 65
A blue-robed goddess
    Out of the night.

Crowned with the stars,
    Her feet on flowers
Her dark eyes shining 70
    With beauty bright.

And without ceasing
    She breathed out blessing
Upon all creatures
    Brought to birth. 75

Those that could kill me
    With love did fill me!
No thing was hateful
    In all the earth.

Quenched was my yearning 80
    And I all burning
To fall before them
    In sacrifice.

Persephone!
    I gazed on thee 85
And thy great Mother
    With open eyes!

Persephone!

(**Orpheus** *observes for the first time that he is surrounded by a ring of listening animals.*)

Encircled by my listeners once again!
Dear creatures, sitting crouching at my feet, 90
Dear friends, who come to help me ease my pain
With your still presence! Say, what can I do?
You have saved me from madness. My pent soul
You have set free, calling it out of prison
Into you on the wings of its own song; 95
What would you have me do in recompense?

How shall I serve you? Answer me!
    They cannot answer me—save with my voice.
It is their bridge. I will sing to them again.
And listen while I sing:
(*Sings:*)
                              Eurydice!   100
Smooth-gliding nymph, bright wife,
Who floated down the river of my life
Clothed in her beauty's seamless vesture
And slipping liquid without pause
From gesture into lovely gesture—   105
Lovely in motion, beautiful in rest—

The Swan
    Proud arched above the waters, breast to breast,
    I float; in my unearthly whiteness
    Gathering the Cloud-gatherer's brightness,
    I become Leda's groom   110
    And fill with dazzling Helen her dark womb.
    I fill with light the light,
    But always cruel night
    Shoots from my frowning forehead looped to kiss
    Itself in the clear water. In cold spite—   115

The Swan & the Serpent (*simultaneously*)
⌈I hiss! I hiss!
⌊You hiss! You hiss!

The Serpent
    In your neck's tortuous length
    Strives Zeus's sinewy strength.
    You become Leda's groom
    And fill with Clytaemnestra her dark womb—   120

The Swan
    Till at the last
    My song is sweet because my life is past.

Orpheus

I hear, O Serpent—and I hear, O Swan!
(Sings:)
    Thine arms about me placed
Melt me in streaming ocean. Mine around thee pressed   125
Draw down my music spirit to the earth
To be the girdle round thy waist—
As ivy round the slender birch-tree clinging—
So we be one flesh, let the spheres cease singing!

The Bull

        Stars cease singing—   130
            Music caught
        Into body—
            Stamp and snort—

        Pulses throb,
            Having new   135
        World to fashion,
            Work to do—

        Master fear!
            Scarlet warns—
        Courage rises—   140
            Lock horns!

        Get kind!
            Chew cud!
        Thicken muscle,
            Milk and blood.   145

        Trust in girth,
            Bones' weight—
        Trust in earth—
            Pan is great!

Orpheus

I hear, oh Bull! But yet—   150

The Ass

An invisible warder keeps placing himself in my track!
They are blind—let them whip me! I feel not the lash,
                let it crack!
No force shall compel me too far! Back! Back!

Orpheus

I hear, oh Ass! Oh obstinately wise!
(*Sings:*)
The iron band across my breast was broken   155
   And for a time deep grief was its own balm.
It was evening; "Orpheus!" my name was spoken;
   "Lift up thine eyes and in the blue find calm!"

The Eagle

I gaze upon the sun. High where I hover
   In the zoned atmosphere he harps and sings   160
Through me, beside me, round me, under and over—
   His Word that weaves about me is my wings.

I rise, I drink of that eternal fountain—
   I swoop—Hahee! I am the eagle, I!—
Low in the vale—then high above the mountain,   165
   To lace with living soul the empty sky.

For, when the Father seeks another bearer
   To raise his chalice to his glorious wine,
Some mortal youth becomes a new sky-farer
   Caught up on strong wings, and those wings
                       are mine!   170

Orpheus

I hear, oh Eagle!
(*Sings:*)
          One came to meet me
            And soft did greet me,
        A blue-robed goddess
           Out of the night.   175

Crowned with the stars,
　　Her feet on flowers,
Her dark eyes shining
　　With beauty bright.

And without ceasing　　　　　　　　　180
　　She poured out blessing
Upon all creatures
　　Brought to birth.

She stilled their needing—

The Lamb

　　Peacefully feeding　　　　　　　　185
My close lips wander
　　Over the earth,

Take in her sweetness—
　　Then in all meekness
Give back to man　　　　　　　　　　190
　　His Mother's wealth.

I keep back nothing,
　　Give first my clothing
To part among them
　　And last myself.　　　　　　　　　195

Orpheus
I hear, oh Lamb!
You creatures—helpless creatures—I am full of pity,
Pity for the dumb pain behind your eyes!
I desire nothing for myself. No! No!
Nothing for Orpheus. Oh, I am on fire　　　200
That burns and scorches not! I thrive upward!
I could be Semele and not die. Oh Zeus!

The Nightingale
　　Tereu! Tereus! Tereus!
　　　　Philomela! Philomela!
　　Of my own vile abuse　　　　　　205
　　　　Forlorn bewailer,

Wove in rich tapestry
    My own sad story,
Sister, to send to thee,
    Not for vainglory.   210

A candle clear and small
    Shows through the night
By shadows on the wall
    Its constant light.

So Philomela's song,   215
    As once her art,
Is Tereu Tereu, Procne's bitter wrong,
    Not her own smart.

Drawn moan and hurrying jets
    Pour from my tree;   220
My woe never forgets
    Procne Procne.

Orpheus

I hear, oh Nightingale!
You beasts—oh, you all tell me different things:
Speak, one of you with more authority;   225
Which way am I to turn? What shall I do?

The Lion

Lift up, oh lover, thy heart; let it carry thee
Manfully over the river of death!
Stride into Taenarus! Out upon Cerberus!
Ride on the enemy, rush to the innermost: 230
Fall at the feet of the seat of Persephone
    Pour her the gift of thy rhythmical breath!

Lift up, oh lover, thy heart: into Erebus
    Courage shall carry thee, riding on blood.
Listen in faith to thy heart—   235

Orpheus

Oh Lion, cease! You have mistook your man:
I am not one to wear the lion's skin.

It is not, and it cannot be, my way.
Besides, you bid me listen to my heart
As to an oracle—what folly!   240
It tells me different things at different times.
First to stay weeping by my darling's tomb,
Then to become a priest, and then to seek
The Maenads in their orgies—why, my heart
Is no more one, one guide, one guardian   245
Than you have all one voice. Have you one voice?
Oh then speak out and tell me what to do—
Oh speak!

All the Animals
    Help us, oh Orpheus!

Orpheus
        How?

All the Animals
          Seek out
In Hades' realm her whom thou know'st on earth,
Our mother and our queen, Persephone.   250

Orpheus
Strange counsel, when I bade you—Oh, I will!
Eurydice—oh, whither am I led?
I follow—follow whom? Art thou my friend
Or my own soul made visible to haunt me?
I think I am alone . . . Persephone!   255

(The fire dies down, as **Orpheus** *rises to his feet, and the animals
are no longer visible.)*

The Nightingale *(offstage)*
    Drawn moan and hurrying jets
     Pour from my tree;
    My woe never forgets
     Procne Procne.

— Curtain —

Act III Scene i

*(The Realm of **Hades**, brightly lit. On one side **Sisyphus** rolls up a slope a stone, which constantly returns to him. In the centre the **Danaïds** pass briskly to and fro, each carrying a pitcher in one hand. On the other side **Tantalus** is seated: a bunch of grapes and a cup of water continually approach and recede from his lips. All are in chains.)*

*(Enter **Hades** on a higher level; he speaks into a concealed microphone and his voice issues from an amplifier.)*

Hades

Stop!
You loyal shades, all busily employed
About your everlasting tasks — avoid!
That pleasing point of time again draws near
When Hades condescends to incline his ear   5
And all are free, and all are bound by rule,
To voice the bliss of which their hearts are full.
Speak, each of you in turn: —

Sisyphus

Regular rolls my stone, loud my chain clanks,
Sisyphus' bosom swells with heartfelt thanks   10
To thee, oh Master of the world's whole wealth,
Less careful of thy gold than of my health,
Rich without labour, who didst yet invent
Employment, so that I might be content:
Hail, Hades!   15

First Danaïd

New draughts we fetch, new draughts fresh from
                         the spring.

Second Danaïd
And each new draught the very latest thing!

Third Danaïd
Hail, empty pitchers, filling up our lives!

Fourth Danaïd
Hail, sacred right to be unfaithful wives!

First Danaïd
We hate hypocrisy, humbug and cant.   20

Second Danaïd
We spend our whole time getting what we want.

Third Danaïd (*setting down her pitcher*)
Oh, Thou who freed our heads of useless weight!
(*She stands erect and, with a grimace, raises both hands above her head, palms inward, as though to steady a pitcher resting on it.*)

Fourth Danaïd
And kept us slim and kept us up to date!

All
Hail, Hades!

Tantalus
With panting passionate devotion burns   25
Tantalus towards that God from whom he learns
How to extract such lasting sweets of sense
From the nice threshold of experience;
To cultivate the green and tender shoot
Of passion, and arrest the dying fruit;   30
To approach fruition, but avert it—just—
And swoon eternal in the lap of lust;
To store the thrill, to lick the prurient lip
In one long squirm of being about to sip!
Hail, Hades!   35

Hades (*speaking as before*)
    Hail Hades! So too must my greeting be.
    Am I not you, dear Shades? Are you not me?
    Your servant-master you unite to bless
    With love and praise—he looks for nothing less.
    Take back that love—and so your hearts will prove   40
    How Hades' bosom swells with—
    (*Howling offstage*)
                              Down Cerberus!
    Cerberus! Down Cerberus! Cerberus! Down Cerberus!
    I say the love in your own hearts must prove
    How Hades' bosom swells with answering love!
    Proceed then—but reflect: though out of view,   45
    I still hear all you say, see all you do.
    (*Exit*)

(**Sisyphus**, **Tantalus**, *and the* **Danaïds** *resume their movements.*)

Orpheus (*offstage. During the song he enters.* **Sisyphus** *gradually ceases moving and stands listening, spellbound.*)
        Persephone!
    Goddess and Guardian have my soul
        In thy safe keeping!
        Persephone!   50
      I have called on thee
      Waking and sleeping.
        Persephone!
    The breath of mortals syllabling thy name
    Streams forth from Earth, like the autumnal flame   55
      From opening pods,
    When the globed fruit forms naked and all whole
      Drops towards the nether gods—
        Persephone!
    (*To* **Sisyphus**:)
    Friend, what do you there?   60

Sisyphus
    Regular work. Your song still fills the air.

Orpheus
What purpose will it serve when it is done?

Sisyphus
I thank my God it never will be done.

Orpheus
What purpose does it serve, then, in the doing?

Sisyphus
Its own; my happiness; and Hades' will.   65

Orpheus
How is it then you stop and talk to me?

Sisyphus
Your song reminded me of other things:
There was a country . . .
(He falls into a reverie and remains silent.)

Orpheus *(stepping past* **Sisyphus** *towards the* **Danaïds,** *and
    singing. During the song the Danaïds gradually cease moving
    and stand listening to him.)*
            Persephone!
Mother and Maiden — and my steadfast goal!   70
            Persephone,
        Mistress of night and death!
            Persephone,
        I have felt thy breath
When the night cometh after day hath been   75
And the bright manifold of heard and seen,
            The garish world,
Seeps through my closing eyes into my soul,
            To bloom there furled —
            Persephone!   80

First Danaïd
Whose was that voice singing a kind of hymn?

Second Danaïd *(to* **Orpheus***:)*
We have not stopped because we wish to hear.

Third Danaïd
What is there in your past that makes you sing?

Orpheus
My Mother's milk was Hippocrene's spring.

The Danaïds
His mother's milk!   85
(They giggle.)

Fourth Danaïd
We thought it sounded somewhat out of date!

First Danaïd
Poor soul! try something fresher! Drink from this!

(Several offer him their pitchers.)

Orpheus
Ladies, I thank you heartily, I will.
But this is empty! So is this! And this!

Second Danaïd
Oh, that's because we left off keeping on.   90

Third Danaïd
You see, the pitchers are all full of holes.

Fourth Danaïd
That's why the water keeps so pure and fresh.

Orpheus
But how do you contrive to drink of it?

First Danaïd
We don't. We have the right to carry it.

Orpheus
Carry it where?

First Danaïd
To carry it, you know!   95

Orpheus
Who are you?

Second Danaïd
We are called the Danaïds.

Orpheus
What did you do then, when you were alive?

Third Danaïd
We killed our husbands on our wedding night,
All of us all of them.

Orpheus
For what vile crime?

Fourth Danaïd
To make quite sure that there would be no children.   100

Orpheus
Yes. I had heard . . . Mnemosyne!
I called on thee amid the Nereids once,
So help me now again!
(To the **Danaïds:**)   Can you recall
The *taste* of water?

First Danaïd
Taste?

Second Danaïd
Has it a taste?

Orpheus
>   Remember! Close your eyes! Cupped hands—cool
>   tongue—   105

Third Danaïd *(dreamily)*
>   There was a stream ran through my father's garden . . .

*(The other **Danaïds** close in around her, murmuring eagerly.)*

Orpheus *(stepping past the **Danaïds** towards **Tantalus** and*
>   *singing.* **Tantalus** *ceases moving and stands listening.)*
>   Persephone!
>   I am come alive into the place of death.
>   Persephone!
>   Receive my anxious breath   110
>   Into the living mystery of thy name!
>   Persephone!
>   I came alone,
>   I left the good beasts and their bodies warm;
>   Their breath and friendly eyes   115
>   I lost by sacrifice—
>   Oh then, save me from harm!
>   Be near me to lift me from despair—
>   Guide me back whole into the upper air,
>   Persephone!   120

Tantalus *(recovering himself and beginning his movements as*
>   *before:)*
>   To approach fruition, but avert it—just—
>   And swoon eternal in the lap of lust,
>   To store the thrill, and lick the prurient lip—

Orpheus
>   Fool, when you *know* that you will never sip!

Tantalus
> To know what truths to pick and which to leave 125
> Is poesy—some call it make-believe.
> This is the poetry of life—to get
> Anticipation sifted from regret:
> To look before and never look behind,
> Chew the sweet kernel and eschew the rind . . . 130
> I cannot keep it up! Oh, misery!
> Oh singer, there are live coals in my breast!
> You have made me remember.

Orpheus
>   Why, poor soul,
> I meant no harm to you.

Tantalus
>   Sing, sing again!
> Tantalus! Tantalus! I was a man! 135

Orpheus (*beginning to sing:*)
> Persephone—

The Voice of Hades (*from the Amplifier:*)
> To approach fruition, but avert it—just—
> And swoon eternal in the lap of lust,
> To store the thrill, to lick the prurient lip . . .

Tantalus (*reluctantly*)
> In one long squirm of being about to sip. 140
> (*Shrieks with agony.*)

Sisyphus, *the* **Danaïds**, *and* **Tantalus** (*begin to move again,
> as before, reciting simultaneously:*)
> Regular rolls my stone . . .
> New draughts we fetch . . .
> To store the thrill . . .

Orpheus (*loudly and commandingly*)
> Stop!

Scene i

(All cease moving.)

Orpheus *(like one in a nightmare:)*
Down, mounting horrors! Monstrous shapes and
sounds!
Persephone! You cannot hide her from me!
Ho! Phantoms, back, I say! Persephone!   145

*(The shades fall back on each side, disclosing, in a brighter but
softer light, at the back of the stage,* **Eurydice** *standing asleep.
Immediately behind her, but on a slightly higher level,*
Persephone. **Orpheus** *walks up stage towards them, with
bowed head, as if groping his way:)*

I feel the light upon my dazzled eyes.
I dare not look.
(Kneels without looking up.)
Lady, all blest and blessing—at thy feet
I cast myself in humblest sacrifice.
I, living, on the altar of the dead;   150
Oh fold me in the shelter of thy robe
Against the horrors that assail my heart.
(Looking up:)
Eurydice! Oh unbelievable!
Floods of forgotten hope roar through my heart—
Oh honey hidden in the heart of gall!   155
Horrors! What horrors? Why, we are alone here!
Eurydice—dear Shade—Eurydice!
Smooth-gliding nymph, bright wife,
Eurydice!

*(***Eurydice*** does not stir.)*

Orpheus *(passionately:)*
Eurydice, awake! Eurydice!
*(***Orpheus*** rises to his feet and steps back a pace.)*

Persephone
Beware!

(**Orpheus**, *in fear and trembling, reaches out his hand towards* **Eurydice**. *As he does so,* **Persephone** *covers her face.*)

The Voice of Hades (*from the Amplifier:*)
　　　What ails my love?

Orpheus (*touching* **Eurydice** *and starting violently:*)
　　　　　　　　　　　Warm!　　　　　　　　　　160
　　　(*He drops his lyre, which breaks in two.*)

Eurydice
　　　Stars moving through a solemn saraband
　　　All in the light of day; no, they are men,
　　　Tall men and goddesses, bowing and passing
　　　And loving one another with their eyes!
　　　And I will join them and be one of them:　　　165
　　　I come—ah! how did I not see it there
　　　Yawning betwixt me and the shining ones?
　　　The chasm! The chasm! I am afraid. I thought
　　　I had died already. Is not once enough?
　　　I will look up to them . . . the vision fades.　　170
　　　It fades.
　　　(*Opening her eyes:*)
　　　　　　　Where am I? Who are these? Orpheus!

(*As* **Eurydice** *raises her arms to embrace* **Orpheus**, *attendants step forward from each side and fasten chains on them.*)

Persephone
　　　Break off these chains! But break them off, I say!
　　　I claim this spirit for Elysium!
　　　Hades! Help, Hades!

Hades (*enters*)
　　　My Queen, my love, though absent, I have heard　　175
　　　Where I was seated, every single word.
　　　Each stir, each breath, by secret stringy nerves
　　　Has reached my throne.

(Howling offstage)

Cerberus, quiet! Down, you swine, down! Lie down!
                I know what each deserves.
No, do not interrupt! We may agree   180
Without a quarrel still. No, pardon me!
In the first place I formally deny
That souls have rights at all. But secondly
I heard one singing; it was not alone
The shrill, the blinding sweetness of his tone   185
(Though this was much), the shape too of the sound
Found favour, as it rang from roof to ground:
To make the air of Hell sigh with *your* name
Gave him (I do confess it) a strong claim,
In short it melted me. And for his pains   190
I give *him* leave to break the Nereid's chains.

Persephone

I grudge you not your reasons and your rules.
She will be free to join the blessed spirits,
As I foretold at first that she would be.

Hades

As you foretold at first! Quite free to come   195
And go betwixt here and Elysium.
(To **Orpheus***:)*
Well, will you set her free?

(Orpheus *breaks the chain from* **Eurydice***. They embrace.)*

Thirdly—if she prefers, not otherwise
(Her freedom once again I emphasize)—
If she prefers to seek the upper air,   200
Nothing shall hinder her from going there . . .
Only—if such her choice she must remain
There, and then *here*—and never seek again
Admission to Elysium—

Persephone

                What is this?

Hades

Unless she shall approach the gates of bliss   205
With her beloved Orpheus at her side:
Then, and then only, shall those gates stand wide.
(Exit)

Persephone

Be not deceived when Death pretends to offer life!

Eurydice

Eurydice was, is, and shall be Orpheus' wife.

Persephone

I see the choice is made! Well, listen then: 210
Orpheus, who summoned me so piously;
Eurydice, so helpless in my charge
Till but a moment back. This God of death
Is keener than you know, malevolent
And omnipresent; even when you embrace,   215
Remember he is with you in your arms,
Orpheus, and in your arms, Eurydice.

Eurydice

I fear!

Orpheus

Teach us to overcome him in your strength!

Persephone

Orpheus!

Orpheus

         Lady!

Persephone

               Eurydice!

Eurydice

I hear.   220

Persephone

Approach. Give me your hand in mine, and yours.
(*To* **Orpheus***:*)
Is it your will to serve this other soul?

Orpheus

I do affirm it is my constant will.

Persephone (*to* **Eurydice***:*)

Is it your will to serve this other soul?

Eurydice

I do affirm it is my constant will.   225

Persephone

Orpheus, to conquer death, you must return,
Following Eurydice, back to these realms
And she may guide you to Elysium;
But first you must go back up to the world,
To do and suffer many things alone —   230

Orpheus

Alone?

Persephone

Alone with her, who is a part of you,
You part of her.

Orpheus

We shall dare all together.

Persephone

Yes, but you will not see her all the while,
She will not pose for you to gaze on her.   235
You will think you have lost her. Are you strong
As you are musical?

Eurydice

>   Orpheus, Orpheus,
> You will be near to me through doubt and dark!

Orpheus

> Eurydice!

Persephone

>   Come then, leave gazing on her
> And do as I shall bid you; much depends   240
> Upon the conduct of your journey back,
> Being the first thing that you have to do.
> I will go on before; follow me, Orpheus,
> And fix your gaze upon me: do not stop
> Or turn or look behind. Eurydice   245
> Will follow you, and so we reach the Light.

(They follow her as bidden. As she reaches the exit, **Persephone** *turns and addressses* **Orpheus***:)*

> Orpheus, the broken pieces of the chain
> Divided by the magic of your singing
> Lie ready to your hand; links forged in Hell
> Are quick to arrest and weighty to retain: 250
> Take one of them and bear it back with you
> Into the life that flows and flows away,
> You may have need of it.

Orpheus *(stooping and picking up a broken piece of the chain)*

> Lead on, lead on, divine Persephone!

The Voice of Hades *(from the Amplifier:)*

> Lead on, lead on, divine Persephone!   255
> But Orpheus, listen: on Eurydice
> Turn not to look! One single furtive glance
> Shall rob her wholly of this final chance
> To find her way back to the upper air—
> I gave it, I will take it back, I swear.   260

I would have left them free, officious Queen,
To guide themselves—*you* chose to intervene.
Take therefore as a gift from Hades' hands
This sanction making law of your commands.
You urged them—I *compel* them, to be free: 265
Lead on, lead on, divine Persephone!

(Exeunt, one by one, **Persephone, Orpheus, Eurydice.**
Sisyphus, *the* **Danaïds,** *and* **Tantalus** *resume their occupa-*
tions.)

—*Curtain*—

Scene ii

(Another part of Hades.)

Ascalaphus *(offstage)*
Tu wit! tu woo!

Hades *(enters, looking up)*
Work for you here, Ascalaphus. Now hark!
Cease your bird noises and attend and mark:
You shall transform yourself to a weak wraith
Of this same Nereid and abuse *his* faith,   5
Appear to him —

Ascalaphus *(offstage)*
       My Lord, how can this be?
If I appear before his startled eyes
Like one who walks *behind* him, my disguise
Will not deceive. All will be thrown away.

Hades
Most true, I had forgot — some other way —   10
The Queen protects his eyes; well then, his ear —
You can assume her voice? Quick, let me hear!

Ascalaphus *(offstage, imitating* **Eurydice***:)*
Orpheus, Orpheus! Be true to me, be true!
Alas, I am forsaken . . .

Scene ii

Hades
That will do!
Fly after them! But one thing more, good spy!   15
Ere you start working, give one clear owl-cry
And I will hear and put my cunning in you
To teach you what to say.

(The stage darkens. During the ensuing lines at first
Persephone *and afterwards* **Orpheus** *dimly appear Left and*
move across to Right. Exit **Persephone** *Right. Just before*
Orpheus *has finished crossing the stage,* **Eurydice** *enters Left.*
Both come to a standstill.)

Orpheus
Lead us, oh star-crowned goddess, Queen of death and
night,
Across the dreadful threshold swung twixt dark and
light.   20

Eurydice
Invisible, behind thee, ever treads more near
Eurydice, thine own one: falter not, nor fear!

Orpheus
I see thee not, Eurydice, and art thou there?

Eurydice
And seest thou thy heart, and seest thou the air?

Orpheus
I see thee not, Eurydice, art thou my wife?   25

Eurydice
Thy light, thy strength, thy soul, thy very self, thy life.

Orpheus
I see thee not, Eurydice—

Eurydice

For we are one—
Two sounds that form one word, two strings that sound
one tone,
One in divine Persephone, on whom we gaze,
One in her blessing on us and one in her praise.   30

Orpheus

I see a pale grey glimmer fall athwart our way—
I think it is the faint tip of the flame of day:
It brightens—ah!

Eurydice

What startles thee? What may this be?

Orpheus

Persephone! Persephone! Persephone!
Our guardian, our guide, our rock amid the shades—   35
Her voice replies no more: her form in daylight fades.
Oh Bull, stamp in my blood! Roar, Lion, in my heart,
That Orpheus may find strength to play his constant
part!

Ascalaphus (*offstage*)

Tu wit! tu woo!
(*Imitating* **Eurydice:**)
Orpheus is strong, so strong he has no need of me!   40

Orpheus

What words are these? Our hope hangs on my
constancy—

Ascalaphus (*offstage, imitating* **Eurydice:**)

Cold constancy! There was a time when thy love
burned.
Thou wast not constant in those days with thy back
turned!

Scene ii

Orpheus
Oh love, love, what then wouldst thou have me do or
be?

Ascalaphus (*offstage, imitating* **Eurydice***:*)
Only this one thing, Orpheus—turn thy face to me!   45

Orpheus
She faints—(Oh fool, fool, blindly trudging on!) I must
Comfort her—turn to her . . . If I do, she is lost!
Mnemosyne! Who am I? I am riven apart!
What shall I do? What shall I do?

Ascalaphus (*offstage, imitating* **Eurydice***:*)
                              Look in thy heart
And do its present bidding, and that shall be right.   50

Orpheus
No. I obey the goddess in my heart's despite.
On, on! How lonely now, how desolate the vale!

Ascalaphus (*offstage, imitating* **Eurydice***:*)
Alas, how far away still sounds the nightingale!

The Nightingale (*faintly*)
                    Drawn moan and hurrying jets
                         Pour from my tree,   55
                    My woe never forgets
                         Procne, Procne.

Orpheus
Forget? Am I forgetting, in the harsh false name
Of gods and duty, her for whom alone I came?
Mnemosyne! Who am I? I am riven apart!   60
What shall I do? What shall I do?

Ascalaphus (*offstage imitating* **Eurydice***:*)
                              Obey thy heart!

Orpheus
> I will obey the goddess—"I"? What I or me
> Is not my heart?
> *(He turns)* Eurydice! Eurydice!

(Arms appear and pull her back into the wings.)

> My own! My own! Oh snatching arms! Oh hideous
> shades!
> Her voice replies no more, her form in darkness fades!

— Curtain —

Act IV Scene i

*(The source of the river Peneus in the vale of Tempe. The curtain rises discovering **Aristaeus** standing or kneeling before a deep pool, formed by the springs at the source of the river.)*

Aristaeus

Mother Cyrene, great Mother Cyrene,
Thou region spirit of this crystal source,
Whence old Peneus, fountain of our being,
Pours forth his life and flows and flows away—
Mother Cyrene, hear me, hear me, hear me!   5
Why didst thou give me life against my will—
Life everlasting, if their tale were true?
And I cannot even keep myself alive!
Why did they make me hopeful of the skies,
Saying my natural father is Apollo,   10
Training me to the service of his altar
With toil and trouble at the hives all day?
"To draw the strands of his bright hair," they said,
"To focus glory into taste," they said,
"To charm the liquid light from far and wide   15
Into the golden wonder of the comb."
Lies—lies! All lies! The pedagogue—the priests!
There is no solid ground beneath the feet
Of prudent, righteous, and industrious men!
    Oh, Mother, Mother, I have lost them all   20
Dropping to earth, not singly but in swarms,
Like rotten clusters from a yellowing tree!
Drought and disease! The vaulted hives like tombs,
Empty and silent—all my bees! all gone!
    They might have killed me when they killed my son!   25
    Oh, you have been too kind! Burn down my sheds!

Root up my trees and trample on my crops
And make a special culture of black bugs
To gorge upon my vines! Oh Mother, Mother!
Empty and silent—all my bees! all gone!   30
    Mother Cyrene, great Mother Cyrene,
Mother Cyrene, hear me! help me! hear me!
(After a pause:)
I fear this place! I speak into the water,
But things of earth are near. Who listens there?
They are all round. Who listens there? Who mocks?   35

The nymph, **Arethusa** *(rising from the pool, to* **Cyrene**,
below:)
Sister, you heard aright. It is your son
Standing in tears upon our Father's banks
Calling you by harsh names—and seeking help
From the eternal fountain of his being—
Unhappy Aristaeus!

Cyrene *(offstage)*
             Bring him down!   40
Being a man he shall converse with gods.
Make room, oh waters now! heap yourselves back
Into two hills! Peneus' flood, obey!

(Enter a **Satyr***)*

Satyr *(to* **Aristaeus***:)*
Stay! Are you a mortal man?

Arethusa *(to* **Aristaeus***:)*
Your mother calls. Follow! Follow me down!   45
(Exit)

Aristaeus *(to* **Satyr***:)*
I am about to learn. Mother, I come!
(Exit)

Scene i

Satyr
Evoe! Evoe! Evoe!

*(A wild throng of **Maenads** emerge from hiding and swirl to and fro. At length they divide into three groups and begin to chant:)*

First Group
Zeus-begotten!

Second Group
                    Iacchus! Iacchus!
    Io!

Third Group
        By Titans torn,

First Group
    Torn to pieces; nearly forgotten,

Second Group
                Io!

Third Group
                    And still unborn!   50

First Group
    From side—

Third Group
            Whose?

First Group
                Zeus's.

Second Group
                        Iacchus! Iacchus!

First Group
> To womb—

Third Group
>> Whose?

First Group
>>> Semele's.

Third Group
> Earth-born!

Second Group
>> Wine-god!

First Group
>>> God of juices!

Second Group
> Iacchus! Io! Iacchus! Iacchus!

Third Group
> Tamer of grapes and bees!   55

All
> Iacchus io Iacchus!
> Iacchus! Iacchus io!

*(The **Maenads** break up and again rush to and fro, eventually pressing in a throng round the **Satyr**.)*

Maenads
>> Do the Thing!
> The Thing! The Thing! Do the Thing! The Thing!
> Do the Thing!

*(The **Satyr** holds up his hand, and the **Maenads** gradually fall back in a rough semicircle with the **Satyr** in the midst.)*

Satyr (*putting on ridiculous airs*)
    What! I am Zeus; the clouds I gather:
    Back! Stand back, for the great All-Father!   60
    Goddesses—nymphs—where find I one
    To fix my wandering fancy on?

First Maenad (*advancing to the middle*)
    Stepping alone on the flowery floor—
    Very demure, very demure—
    I am divine Persephone.   65
    When will my Lover look on me?

Satyr
    Upon your lips I print my kiss.

    (*They embrace, amid ribald applause.*)

First Maenad (*kissing him warmly*)
    And I do this! And this! And this!
    (*She lies down and produces a straw doll, which she holds up
    to him.*)
    See! I have born a babe to Zeus!

Second Maenad (*stepping forward*)
    I am great Hera!

Satyr (*grimacing*)
               Here's the deuce!   70

Second Maenad
    Show me the darling!
    (*Takes the doll.*)   There you are!
    (*Tosses it to the* **Maenads.**)

The other Maenads
    We are the Titans. Ha, ha, ha!
    Seize it! Tear it! Toss it about!
    Worry it! Pluck the red heart out!

(They tear the straw doll to pieces and fling the straw about. A red rose drops out of it, which the **Satyr** *picks up.)*

Satyr

Within my side this heart, still warm   75
I'll hide, to shelter it from harm.

(Meanwhile the **Maenads** *pick up the straw and one of them fashions it into a doll again.)*

Satyr *(putting on his airs again)*

I am great Zeus; the clouds I gather:
Rum dum dum for the great All-Father!
Goddesses—maidens—seek I one
To shower my fiery favours on.   80

Third Maenad *(advancing)*

I am a mortal maiden pure—
Very demure—very demure—
Cadmus's daughter, Semele:
What if a God should stoop to me?

Satyr

Upon your lips I print my kiss.   85
(Kissing her by force.)

Third Maenad

Who is it who has dared do this?
Presumptuous man—expect the rod—
(Starts.)
Whom do I see?

All the Maenads

        The God! The God!
The Flame! The Thunderer! Zeus! Zeus!

Third Maenad
>Why dost thou come as mortals use? 90
>Come to me, dear, tomorrow night
>Clothed in thy glory and thy might—
>Tunic of azure, vest of gold—

Satyr *(approaching her)*
>Poor foolish maiden . . . I come . . .
>*(Towers above her, and at the same time hands her the rose.)*

All *(shouting suddenly at the top of their voices:)*
>BEHOLD! 95

Third Maenad *(falling to the ground and after a pause holding*
>*up the straw doll, which has been given to her.)*
>Scorched and blasted! The Sky all flame
>Was thy father, child; I name thy name:—
>*(She collapses.)*

All *(shouting)*
>Dionysus!

Satyr *(taking the doll in his arms, while one of the **Maenads***
>*squeaks to imitate a baby crying)*
>Poor pretty thing! Did they make it wink?
>What was it crying for?

Maenad *(in a squeaky voice for the baby)*
>   A drink! 100

(All laugh.)

Satyr
>Give it some water then.

*(A **Maenad** fetches water and makes as if to give it to the doll. A*
noise of spluttering.)

>   Oh dear!

Not what it wanted at all, I fear!
Semele's Son, the juice must first
Work in earth that shall quench thy thirst,
And thou shalt wake it; for men shall twine,   105
By thee instructed, the fruitful vine,
And the grape shall swell and there cometh wine!
Semele's Son, the Earth shall make
Smooth sweet liquor, thy thirst to slake.
By thee instructed the men shall know   110
How to hoard what the bees bestow,
And the hive shall hum and the honey flow.

First Maenad

That is enough! Now stop the Thing!

Second Maenad

Where is the man you swore to bring?

Satyr

I found one here, but he would not stay;   115
See now, another one comes this way:

Third Maenad

His mouth is mine,

Fourth Maenad

His cheeks,

Fifth Maenad

His eyes!

Sixth Maenad

I'll kiss his neck,

First Maenad

His shoulders,

Second Maenad

Thighs.

Scene i

Third Maenad
  Back,

Fourth Maenad
    Belly,

Fifth Maenad
      Buttocks,

Sixth Maenad
        Knees,

First Maenad
          Hocks,

Second Maenad
            Side . . .

Satyr
  Hush! or you'll frighten him! All hide!   120
  Oh, it's the lonely one who sings—
  What if he scorns you all, poor things!

Third Maenad
  Scorns? What manner of man is this?

Satyr
  Says he's forgotten how to kiss.

Fourth Maenad
  We shall remind him—

Fifth Maenad (*raising her foot*)
      Maenad trips—   125

Sixth Maenad
  Maenad smothers him, lips on lips—

First Maenad
Maenad clutches him round the waist—

Second Maenad
Artemis keep all maidens chaste!

Satyr
You laugh—but you may lose your pains.

Third Maenad
Is it water that flows through his veins?   130

Satyr
Some say so—others . . . come more near—
They say—this in your private ear
(*Whispers.*)

(*The* **Maenads** *howl with execration and fury.*)

Fourth Maenad
Vile!

Fifth Maenad
Monstrous!

Sixth Maenad
                    Shall such flesh still live?
We'll take all him he will not give!

Third Maenad
His mouth is mine!

Fourth Maenad
                    His cheeks!

Fifth Maenad
                                        His eyes!   135

90

Scene i

Sixth Maenad
I'll suck his neck!

First Maenad
                    His shoulders!

Second Maenad
                                        Thighs!

Third Maenad
Back,

Fourth Maenad
    Belly,

Fifth Maenad
            Buttocks,

Sixth Maenad
                        Knees,

First Maenad
                    Hocks,

Second Maenad
                                Side.

Satyr
Hush! You are warning him! Quick! All hide!

*(The **Maenads** scatter and conceal themselves. The **Satyr** seats himself at one side.)*

*(Enter **Orpheus**. He still carries the broken piece of chain instead of his lyre. Without seeing the **Satyr** he seats himself and begins to sing sentimentally.)*

Orpheus

Forever are you mine, Eurydice,
    Inexorable Lethe's icy stream   140
That reaves the lover from his lost Lady—
    How shall be drowned your image in my dream?
(Pause)
Do you remember still, my dear, my dear?
    All the passionate names you heard me sing?
Does your dead heart cry, when my voice comes clear: 145
    This is the man who called me "smooth-gliding"?

The pleasant places where we planned to meet,
    The brave clean laughter and the splendid days—
Intimacies intolerably sweet—

Satyr *(singing)*

    Though pork and greens are better in some ways!   150

Orpheus *(turning with a start)*

    You mock at beauty—well, it is your trade.

Satyr

    Oh beauty, thou art beautiful and sweet!

Orpheus

    Why do you mock me in my wretchedness?

Satyr

    Hearing a false note makes me laugh, like tickling.

Orpheus

    What is there false in singing my lost love?   155

Satyr

    Because true sweetness always tastes of earth.

Orpheus

    Oh, I will try no more to cheat myself!
    Oh, Faun, I have forgotten how to sing!
    Say what you mean! Has grief no taste of earth?

Scene i

Satyr
Earth changes every moment, earth grieves not,   160
Though nothing lasts, nor comes the same again.

Orpheus
There is no lilt without the same again.

Satyr
Poet, who never listened to the birds!

Orpheus
Grief suffered is the bones of constancy.

Satyr
Constancy—I have heard the word before.   165
Like loyalty—the thing they do in Hell—
Loyal to Hades they, and here on earth
You men must all be loyal to the past
And go about like dogs wearing a chain,
Pretending that to-day is yesterday!   170
True loyalty is living with the earth.
Why, man, I see your chain there in your hands!
Throw it away, and be a man indeed!

Orpheus
Faun, you are foolish—you are wise—oh Zeus,
I cannot even speak now like one man!   175
Riven apart! What good has ever come
Keeping the chain? Why then—away with it!
(*Throws it into the water.*)
Weak fool! It was Persephone's command.

Satyr
But try now, Orpheus, if you cannot sing!

Orpheus (*after a pause, intoning solemnly*)
The grandson of Heracles lived comfortably ever after,   180
Eating black-puddings while he watched a trilogy,
Pillowed upon his doxy's ripening bust.

Phoebus Apollo got more marks than Pan.
It was the mastersinger Marsyas who began piercing
The astute projections . . . Pah! 185
(*To the* **Satyr**:)
Well, why do you not mock?

Satyr

You cast away false sweetness with the chain.

Orpheus

Sweetness, perhaps, not falseness. I have done!
The lilt, the lilt is gone, the lilt is gone!

Satyr

Sweetness is never music without strength. 190

Orpheus

What shall I do, oh Faun, what shall I do?

Satyr

Bring sacrifices to the Earth-born God.

Orpheus

Dionysus? Of what is the sacrifice?
Where? How is it performed?

Satyr

I know those that will teach you . . .

Orpheus

Well, speak out! 195

Who are these teachers? Where?

Satyr

I speak of Maenads,

Orpheus

Why of such?

Satyr

                              Whose hair
Floats level in the wind above their bodies'
White rippling waves of passion: at such times
The might of earth is in them. Give them Orpheus!   200

Orpheus

   So, when a swimmer drifts upon a wave,
You say its might is *in* him.

Satyr

                   You split words!
No wonder all the Muses flee away!

Orpheus

   Thoughts may be false as well as sweetness, Faun!
Daughters of Memory have fled from men,   205
But not because their thinking was too straight!

Satyr

   Yet these same Maenads never lost—the lilt.

Orpheus

   Our goat-foot doctor cures unhappy men
By making happy animals!

Satyr

                 You need
Not sneer at beasts, if what they say is true!   210

Orpheus
   What?

*(The **Satyr** approaches and whispers to **Orpheus**.)*

Orpheus *(calmly)*
   The vilest slanders cannot prick despair.

Satyr
Well, have you never wished to?

Orpheus
                  Often.

Satyr
                       Oh,
Cast off your crusting pride, and join the rout!

Orpheus *(shaking his head:)*
It is not and it cannot be my way.   215

Satyr
You are earth. Earth wants earth. Flesh will have flesh.

Orpheus
Somewhere beyond earth. Once—

Satyr
                  What?

Orpheus
                    I know not.

Satyr
"Know not!" "I know not!" Why, you stammering fool,
Do you say you are greater than the God
Who sprang from earth and made the earth his care?   220

Orpheus
I said not so.

Satyr
          Then join his devotees!

Orpheus
I cannot—will not—

Scene i

Satyr

Which?

Orpheus

I do not know.

Satyr
God's blood! This is too much!
(Aside:)   I will be calm!
(To **Orpheus***:)*
Song rises from the beating of the blood!
Then trust in earth—surrender to the blood—   225
Joy will bring back the power of song again.

Orpheus
It may be you are right. I cannot come.

Satyr
Come with us—or say why you cannot come.

Orpheus
My troth is plighted to Eurydice.

A Maenad *(concealed)*
Unnatural!   230

Satyr
To live without joy is to flout the gods.

Orpheus
My joy is buried with Eurydice.

A Maenad *(concealed)*
Blasphemy!

Orpheus
I will be silent, if I cannot sing
Out of my sorrow and my love—

Satyr

You fool!   235

    This parrot-cry of yours has made them mad.

Orpheus

    My sacrifice is to Eurydice.

Satyr

    Your sacrifice will be to Dionysus!
    I wash my hands of you.
    (Raising his voice:)   Heard you all this?

Orpheus

Eurydice!   240

The Maenads *(still concealed)*

    Unnatural! Monstrous! Blasphemy! Flesh! Flesh!

Satyr *(suddenly springing back from* **Orpheus***)*

    And blood! And Blood! Evoe! Evoe!

Maenads

    Iacchus, io iacchus! Iacchus, iacchus io!

(They rush from all sides upon **Orpheus***, who covers his head with his hands.)*

Seize him! tear him! Toss him about!

Worry him! Pluck the red heart out!   245

Orpheus *(sinking to his knees beneath them)*

    Eurydice!

— Curtain —

Scene ii

(As the curtain descends on Scene i, the Chorus begins at once to recite:)

First Chorus
    But Aristaeus on the watery floor
    Stands swaying like a lily-stalk—

Second Chorus
                       a pearl
    Embedded in a solid steep green swirl
    Of waters, whose wide roaring in his ears
    Has robbed him of himself.

First Chorus
                    But Cyrene   5
    Draws near her son and takes him by the hand
    And heartens him,

Second Chorus
              till he begins to see
    The nymphs and naiads, with their rainbow veils,
    Drymo, Phyllodoce, and Beroë
    And Arethusa and Deïopeia,   10
    And many more whose names I cannot tell,
    Sitting and spinning green thread shot with grey,
    Among whom Clymene, with busy wrists,
    Sits telling tales that often make them laugh.

First Chorus
    He strives to speak. Cyrene answers not   15
    But gravely guides his slow bewildered steps
    Into a pumice grotto,

Second Chorus

> seats herself,
> Calls to the nymphs to bring her bread and wine
> And set them on the board.

First Chorus

> Cyrene rises
> To pour new strength into her fainting son,   20
> Pouring libations to Oceanus.

(Curtain rises. The scene is under the river Peneus. **Aristaeus**, **Cyrene**, *and an attendant nymph holding a cup are seen separately within a grotto. Some of the nymphs are without.)*

Aristaeus

> The great deep rises round; I cannot see,
> I cannot feel the ground I stand upon.

Cyrene

> Oceanus, Oceanus!
> Offspring of Earth and Sky,   25
> Horizon-wide,
> Take into thy pure tide
> My dark libation!
> Pour!

(The nymph pours wine from the cup. Music.)

Aristaeus

> I stand beneath all rivers; all are one   30
> Great globe of waters; I am lost in them.

Cyrene

> Oceanus, mighty Oceanus,
> Let mingle with thy brine
> The purple stain of wine!
> Receive from us,   35
> Oceanus,
> Contamination!
> Pour!

Scene ii

(The nymph pours as before. Music.)

Aristaeus
    I am awake. I dimly see above, around,
    High halls and mighty rivers meeting underground.   40

Cyrene
        Oceanus, boundless Oceanus,
      O thou whose living pulse can never stop,
      Let the firm body of each rounded drop
      Diffuse its essence through thy formless
          whole,
      Let man's warm suffering soul,   45
        Enter thy working stream
        And rouse thee from thy dream
           To inspiration!
           Pour!

(The nymph pours as before. Music.)

Cyrene
    The God hears and accepts: I prophesy: 50

Second Chorus *(for* **Cyrene** *inspired, rhythmically)*
    Bowing to the trident, the tritons dance
    And the waves sparkle; wild white horses
    Prance round promontories: Proteus is very old,
    Sitting upon the sea off the shore of Thrace,
    Nine times older than Nereus is he.   55
    What is, what was, what will be he knows.
        Cunning is needed: he knows not that he knows;
    He is all creatures except himself,
    He is life shifting from shape to shape;
    He is life flowing and flowing away.   60
    First you must seize him—fix him into form:
    Fetter will be found for you, forged in Hades,
    Near to where I stand, though I know not where.
    But cease not, oh my son, cease not from gripping:
    The more he changes, chain him still the more: 65

Hold on till the time when he turns again
Back to the form you first found him in.
Then press no more; Proteus will prophesy,
Reach down to the roots of your ruin at last,
And show you a remedy sure and certain.   70

Cyrene
The God has left me. What have I been saying?

Arethusa (*to a group of nymphs at the side, who are busy with
something:*)
Well, let us show it to Cyrene first.
Our sister will know what to do with it.

Cyrene
What is it, Arethusa?

Arethusa
                          Something strange
Phyllodoce found lying on the ground—   75

Cyrene
It speaks into my blood. I know. I know.
As if you had already shown it me,
And I had spoken—I have—said I not:—
"Fetter will be found for you, forged in Hades
Near where I stand." . . . Why do you hold it back?   80
Bring it here: I must give it to my son.

Arethusa
I do not understand you.

Cyrene
                          Show it me!

(**Arethusa** *holds up the head of* **Orpheus**.)

Fetter! This is a man's head. What now?

Arethusa
                                          Ah!

Cyrene
Why do you start?

Arethusa
The thing stirred in my hands.

Cyrene
The lips are moving.

Arethusa
Ah!

The Voice of Orpheus
Eurydice!   85

Arethusa
I am afraid no longer.

Cyrene
Set it down!
It is too holy to be tampered with.
Lay it down gently on the river bed.
Father Peneus will have care of it,
And urge it gently down his winding course   90
Into the bosom of Oceanus.

(**Arethusa** *sets the head down.*)

A Nymph (*to a group of nymphs with her on the other side, who are busy with something:*)
Ugly!

Second Nymph
Jagged and rusty.

Third Nymph
Bury it deep.
Bury it underneath the white clean sand
And let our Father wash it smooth again
For us to dance upon.

First Nymph

But show it first   95
To Cyrene, our sister. Cyrene!

(A nymph holds up the fragment of **Eurydice's** *chain.)*

Cyrene *(to* **Aristaeus***:)*
Behold the fetter!
(To the nymph:)

Bring it here to me.

First Nymph
We love it not. We mean to bury it.

Cyrene
Bring it to me!

(The nymph gives her the chain. To **Aristaeus***:)*

My Son:
(She holds out the chain.)

Take it and use it.

Chorus *(for* **Cyrene***, inspired, who stands holding the chain,
and as if still addressing* **Aristaeus***, but in a prophetic
manner:)*
Grip him! Grasp him! He will grind his teeth,   100
Awake in a wink, working to elude you
By shifting of his shapes. A sheep he will become,
A lion or a bull or a bird beating
With airiest wings, and then air itself,
Then a snake, then an ass, animal or element,   105
A flickering flame, flowing water.
But cease not, oh my Son, cease not from gripping!
The more he changes, chain him still more!

*(***Aristaeus*** takes the chain from* **Cyrene's** *hands.)*

—*Curtain*—

Scene iii

*(Similar to Scene i. **Aristaeus** alone standing in the centre of the stage behind a large recumbent black bull.)*

Aristaeus
The time has come.

Satyr *(entering)*
              Are you a mortal man?

Aristaeus
I am a man. Go, and disturb me not.
I sacrifice . . .
(Starts)   "Are you a mortal man"—
Someone has spoken thus to me before.
You—it was you!

Satyr
            Yes, and thereat you dived   5
Into the river, leaving me alone
Without an answer.

Aristaeus
          Not without a victim!
You and your rabble horde tore limb from limb
Orpheus, the husband of Eurydice.

Satyr
How should you know of this? No trace was left   10
After my maidens took their pleasure of him.
Many animals devoured the severed limbs
Scattered about the ground: his gory head

I took myself and hurled into the stream.
How do you know?

Aristaeus

From Proteus, who knows all.   15

Satyr
But how did you make Proteus tell you all?

Aristaeus
I bound him fast from changing.

Satyr

With your hands?

Aristaeus
No, with a chain my mother found for me,
Forced him to keep a fastened form,
Forced him to prophecy. Reluctantly   20
He told me all the story of those twain,
Eurydice and Orpheus; and because
I, even I, was guilty of their woe,
My bees dropped dead and all my flocks were stricken.
I was grown desperate of a remedy!   25
Proteus divined the anger of the gods,
He bade me choose a black unblemished bull
And in this place, hard by where Orpheus died,
Sacrifice to Eurydice's wronged shade.

Satyr
Evoe!

Aristaeus (*starting up and threatening him with the sacrificial knife*)
Silence! What treachery is here?

Satyr

No harm!   30

Scene iii

Aristaeus

No harm! Were you not signalling to your crew
Of drunken prancing harlots?

Satyr

They are changed.
Since that dread day they tore the Thracian bard
And half devoured his quivering flesh, it seems
Feasting and rioting delight them not.   35
They walk demurely followed by their friends,
The animals.

Aristaeus

Animals?

Satyr

Those that day
Who fed upon his body after them.
Oh Man, that was a holy sight to see:
Different in kind, not growling, without greed   40
They took those dreadful commons. Let them share
The gods' meal also. Quick!
(He beckons to **Maenads** *offstage.)*
My bristling fur
Prompts me of good approaching. Evoe!

(Enter **Maenads***, and after them, the animals as in Act II,
Scene ii.)*

Aristaeus

So be it! Shades of Eurydice, hear my prayer! I have
sinned much. I have caught down the music of the spheres   45
into the mechanic rhythm of my own heightened pulse; I
have surrendered to the clamour of the blood, and all my
strength has been but the alien strength of the lust in me.
Shades of Eurydice, hear my prayer!
(He kneels.)

O bull, willing sacrifice, bound by no thongs upon 50
the altar, wilt thou indeed renounce the thunder of thy
hooves, the coursing of thy blood, thy snorting and paw-
ing upon the ground, thy sitting and the slow pleasant
motion of thy jaws? If not, arise and go. Thou knowest
thou art free! 55

*(A pause. **Aristaeus** raises the knife, to strike.)*

Satyr *(to the **Maenads**:)*
Shout, when the blow falls. Let no groan be heard!

*(All shout as the knife falls. Dead silence. A faint atmospherical
rustling is heard. At length the amplified voice of **Hades** speaks.)*

The Voice of Hades
Back! Back! You shall not pass!

The Voice of Orpheus
                               Hades, our time is come!
We pass, my lady leading, to Elysium.

The Voice of Hades
Think you I shall cease fighting?

The Voice of Eurydice
                               Nay, fight on Hades!
Farewell, I cannot see thee now for clouds of bees. 60
Fight on, fight, hate, devour—and so, even so, shall
                               sweet
Out of the strong come forth, out of the eater meat.

*(During the speaking of the next few lines, the rustling gradually
dies away.)*

The Voice of Orpheus
Thy love breathes in this air; it is so soft and bright.

The Voice of Eurydice
Thy music has gone up from earth into this light.

(From the interior of the bull's carcass a light begins to glow and grows steadily brighter as the scene proceeds.)

Aristaeus
Look, Satyr, look, a light grows in the dark.   65
My prayer is answered. I am saved.

Satyr
                              O hark!

First Maenad
Where are we, Sister, where are we?

Second Maenad
                    I dreamed a horrible dream.

Third Maenad
There sounded a voice which woke me.

Fourth Maenad
The light all strange doth seem.

The Voice of Eurydice
Lo, where the bees stream up through crannies on to
                              earth!

Second Maenad
Evil things were done in my dream, aiai, aiai.   70

The Voice of Orpheus
Their bodies soaked in light, to which thy love gave
                              birth.

First Maenad
Evil things were done in my dream, and the doer was I.

Third Maenad

> There sounded a voice that woke me, a strange voice
> > crying: Sweet
> Out of the strong shall come forth, out of the eater
> > meat.

The Lion

> I am the Lion, the King of beasts; on the mountain-slope, 75
> Roaming at large and swiftly, I followed the antelope.
> I deemed that I had good hunting, I felt my heart
> > rejoice;
> And I was crouched all ready to spring, when I heard
> > that voice:
> I lifted my head and listened: A strange voice crying:
> > Sweet
> Out of the strong shall come forth, out of the eater
> > meat! 80

Aristaeus (*kneeling beside the carcass of the Bull, to the* **Satyr:**)
> > Black and bubbling ferment
> > > Worketh up like yeast
> > Down in the dark entrails
> > > Of the butchered beast.

Satyr

> > > Like the singing sweetness, 85
> > > > Far and faint and deep
> > > Rising round my senses
> > > > As I fall asleep.

> > > Like the slumbrous shimmer
> > > > Heat spreads over things, 90
> > > Hum and whine and buzz
> > > > Innumerable wings.

Scene iii

Aristaeus

> See, ye gods and mortals,
> > Gendered of the warm—
> See the honey-makers,   95
> > Swarm on swarm on swarm.
>
> One mysterious body
> > Of a myriad lives!
> Happy Aristaeus!
> > Overflowing hives!   100

All the Animals

What is here for us? We followed the Lion. The Lion's
> will
Worked in us. Wherefore are we brought hither, oh Man!

Aristaeus

> Be still!
For I hear the voices of gods talking to one another:
The lady Persephone calling across to the great Earth-
> Mother.

The Voice of Persephone

Have I used well, Demeter, the man's good gift of his
> breath?   105

Second Chorus

Thou hast done well, Persephone, I rejoice thou art
> wedded to Death.

The Voice of Persephone

Have I done well, oh Mother, promising much in a sign?

Second Chorus

Thou hast done well, oh Maid, and I hold thy promise
> as mine.

The Voice of Persephone

Shall his agony profit at all? Shall Man at the last be
> whole?

Second Chorus

He shall ascend Parnassus awake and find his soul: 110
Proteus shall work unsleeping for ever, and forms shall
                    flow
As the meanings of words a poet has mastered. It shall
                    be so
That Zeus shall abandon to Cronos the antique starry
                    crown,
And softly out of Olympus the high gods shall come
                    down
Shedding ambrosial fragrance in clouds that for ever
                    abide,   115
And earth shall be covered with blushes and make
                    herself sweet as a bride.
And her light shall be liquid as honey, her air taste good
                    like bread
In the mouths of them that dwell upon earth, and all
                    shall be fed.

— Curtain —

FINIS

PROGRAM NOTE FOR THE ORIGINAL PRODUCTION

The following observations appeared on the Program when ORPHEUS *was first performed, in Sheffield, at the Little Theatre, from the twentieth through the twenty-fifth of September, 1948.*

Most people have heard of the central event in the story of Orpheus and Eurydice. They know of the condition under which he was permitted to rescue his wife from the lower regions and of his failure to observe it. But the surrounding mythology is much less familiar. There is, for instance, nothing in Gluck's lovely opera to suggest that Eurydice was a Nereid. In Virgil's fourth *Georgic* the well-known story occurs as the centerpiece in another story, that of Aristaeus and the loss and restoration of his bees. It is in fact told to Aristaeus by Proteus, when the former consults him to ascertain the cause of the disaster and its proper remedy.

The framework of my play is the whole of the story told by Virgil. The play presents the story primarily for its own sake, but since it is a myth, the true dramatic shape and development lie as much in the sequence of images as in the incidents and characters as such. A single sequence progresses from incidents of which Orpheus is the central figure to others of which Aristaeus is the central figure. One way of putting the matter would be to say that the true *hero* of the play is represented in the persons of both Orpheus and Aristaeus. But now for the story itself.

Eurydice, a Nereid, one of the fifty daughters of the sea-god Nereus, is wooed and won by Orpheus, who is the son of Apollo by the Muse Calliope. Their joy in each other is paradisal, while it lasts, but Orpheus, inevitably, begins to impart to the vaguely conscious water-being, his wife, some of that reflective self-consciousness which made him a musician and poet and without which (as he points out to her) he would never have been able to single her out as his bride. Eurydice learns her lesson with enthusiasm. She even seeks to dwell on ecstatic experience by deliberately interrupting and repeating it, and it is while she has momentarily left Orpheus with this object in view that she is seen and pursued by Aristaeus, another son of Apollo by the water nymph Cyrene. In her flight she is bitten by a serpent and dies.

She is conveyed by Charon to Hades (the name, both of the lower regions and of their tyrannical ruler) but arrives there in a condition of sleep. Hades seeks to awaken her, but it proves impossible. He declares that, when she does awaken, she must be judged and placed in chains like his other subjects. But Persephone, his queen (who is a goddess partly of the nether world and partly of the upper air), insists that when that happens, Eurydice shall be allowed to proceed to Elysium, the abode of the blessed. The dispute is left unresolved.

Crushed by his bereavement, Orpheus seeks consolation in his power of song, and such is the beauty of his music that the birds and wild beasts assemble to listen to it. Beneath its spell they are moved to utter a language which Orpheus is able to understand. It teaches him the beauty and wisdom of renunciation, and he promises, for their sake rather than his own, to visit the realm of Hades, in order to seek the aid of Persephone.

He visits that realm and, expecting to be confronted with Persephone, in fact encounters the shade of Eurydice, whom his voice arouses for the first time from the condition of sleep in which she has been sunken since her death. Her touch reawakens all his renounced personal passion. Chains are at once fastened on Eurydice, against which Persephone protests to Hades. Moved, as he says, by the beauty of Orpheus's song and desirous of pleasing his Queen, Hades agrees to allow Eurydice to return to earth, but he and Persephone together impose on the lovers the condition that Orpheus shall lead the way to the upper air and shall not look back upon Eurydice till the journey is accomplished. With the help of his spy, Ascalaphus (recently transformed by Persephone into an owl), Hades takes care that the poet shall fail to fulfill these terms. Eurydice is snatched back into the shades and Orpheus returns to earth once more alone.

He is no longer followed by the animals. Nature has deserted him, and with dull despair, he finds that even his power of music has gone. He sings, but the songs are banal or sophisticated, and he knows it. The Maenads, followers of the wine-god Dionysus, are incensed alike by his idiotic constancy to the mere memory of Eurydice (which makes him decline the renewal of living inspiration they can offer) and by rumours of his indulgence in unnatural practices. Excited by a piece of crude but all too significant ritual, half serious, half burlesque, as well as by the drunken orgy which preceded it, they fall upon Orpheus and tear him limb from limb.

Meanwhile disaster of a different kind has overtaken Aristaeus. His bees, on which he relied for a livelihood, have all died of famine or disease. Destitute and hopeless, he decides to implore the help of his mother Cyrene, and he visits her accordingly at the source of the sacred river Peneus, where she dwells with her sister nymphs. It was into this river that the Maenads, or the Satyr who led them, had flung the head of the dismembered Orpheus, and when the nymphs discover it there, it utters the name of his beloved. When she has heard Aristaeus' story, Cyrene, after pouring a libation to Oceanus, is able to advise him to consult Proteus, a sea-god older and wiser than Nereus and possessing, like him, the faculty of changing himself into every conceivable shape. Acting upon the sea-god's advice, Aristaeus sacrifices a bull to the shade of Eurydice, and thereupon a miracle is wrought and his bees are restored to him in richer measure than before.

"If bees were always bees and nothing more," as Hades has remarked in Act II, Scene i, that would be all the story, but the bees had a way of carrying sunlight down from the upper air into the nether regions, a process which could end only in breaking down the barrier between the two worlds. It had begun to crumble a little before the story opens—a fact of which both Hades and, in his different way, Charon showed an uneasy awareness. The final choruses suggest that the dykes are down at last, and among them are heard the voices of Orpheus and Eurydice, joyous now, for Orpheus has found again both his music and his beloved.

That is the story, and Eurydice will find this account of it more than enough. Before I add any more, let me emphasise that it is the lady whom I am really concerned to please. If she should be delighted—even satisfied—not otherwise, I shall consider the play a success. The Orpheus in the Spectator's mind will be pondering over a *significatio* or inner meaning of some sort. I must tell him, not that there is no such thing, but that there is no single one. The figures of Greek mythology are so rich in imaginative potentiality that anyone who welcomes a few of them into his own imagination, with its twentieth-century furniture, will find that there is no need to go out of his way to hunt for modern instances and applications. Rather they come crowding so thick and fast that he is positively embarrassed by them. I think, however, that while I was working on this play, the figure of Orpheus came to stand, in some degree, for the practice of reflection on experience and its results. All conscious nature has experiences of pleasure and pain. Man alone can deliberately will the *repetition* of an experience. And repetition, experienced as such, is at the heart, for good and evil, of his faculty of reasoning, and thus makes possible his language, his art, his morality, and indeed his humanity. Yet it is the enemy of life, for repetition is itself the principle, not of life but of mechanism.

A—what shall I say?—a root-concept of this nature has a way of showing its face beneath many widely separated realms of human experience. Especially if you *give* it a face, by allowing it to coalesce with a living figure such as that of Orpheus. I at any rate seemed to see that countenance peeping through such things as: music and poetry, the relation between man and woman, the relation between mankind and the world of nature, the progress or regress of civilisation, the fall of man and his morality, psychology, the history of the Romantic Movement, and the mystery of death and resurrection. And the lacerated look which it wore seemed to me to express the tragedy inherent in human destiny itself. The number "two" was regarded as sacred to the god Hades, and it was perhaps natural that I should conceive the place Hades as the region where the principle of lifeless repetition has triumphed, where Sisyphus's stone rolls back to him with the regularity of clockwork, and where the innocent voluptuousness which Orpheus had awakened in Eurydice, and his own tendency to substitute for her personal "otherness" a mere wraith fabricated by the devil and his own desires, have both been carried by Tantalus to their logical conclusion ("logical" indeed) in sub-humanity. Whether it was equally natural to relate this place as closely as I have done to the *upper* world, as we know it today, the world of our highly abstract and therefore increasingly totalitarian and mechanized civilisation, may be disputed. The play was written before 1939. Those who can accept the convention will, I hope, feel with me that for us too, there are signs, faint enough no doubt, of an imminent crumbling of the stern barrier between that dreary place and what corresponds with the "upper air" of myth.

OWEN BARFIELD

Afterword

Since Mr. Barfield began his Foreword to *Orpheus* with an anecdote of its genesis, it seems fitting, *sub specie polaritatis*, that my Afterword begin with an anecdote of its regeneration. In the summer of 1973, with the aid of a grant from the National Endowment for the Humanities—whose support is here gratefully acknowledged—I was doing some literary research in England. In connection with that project (which was chiefly concerned with the work of C. S. Lewis and J. R. R. Tolkien), I spent more than a week with Owen Barfield, inquiring into Inklings and related matters. During the course of my visit, Barfield's own literary productions came in for a good deal of discussion. But though I made many discoveries—correspondence with C. S. Lewis and others, numerous essays then out of print and not readily available, and a fair amount of unpublished poetry—I learned nothing at all about *Orpheus*. And though I reproach myself for my lack of enterprise, Barfield must share the responsibility, for he scrupulously avoided mentioning any of his fictive offspring. Indeed, his other major early poems, *Riders on Pegasus* and *The Unicorn*, not to mention several other plays, a novel, and a novella, continued to elude my search and are only now being given the attention they deserve.

I came across my first clue to the existence of *Orpheus* only several weeks later, in the Bodleian Library of Oxford University, where I was investigating the miscellaneous correspondence of C. S. Lewis. (The main C. S. Lewis archives are in the Wade Collection of the Wheaton College Library, but the Bodleian has, besides photocopies of the Wade material, a substantial collection of original letters and manuscripts. For making this material available to me, and for assisting my circumlocutious researches, I owe a substantial debt of gratitude to the librarians of the Duke Humphrey Reading Room, and to the Reverend Walter Hooper.) Since I was primarily interested in Tolkien's relation to the Inklings, *via* Lewis, the clue aforementioned almost escaped my notice entirely. In one of Lewis's letters to Barfield, dated December 16, 1947, my attention was briefly captured by the following obscure allusion: "I am delighted about Orpheus." Being unable to make anything of this cryptic aside, I thought little enough about it at the time and merely noted it for future reference.

My first solid lead turned up only two days later, in a photocopy of a letter that Clyde Kilby, then curator of the Wade Collection, had discovered "with other letters attached . . . to Owen Barfield's ms. 'Orpheus.' " The undated letter was, in essentials, the Note on *Orpheus* that is printed on the back cover of the present volume, followed by two postscripts: "Why do I feel a cad to be writing blurbs for you?" and "It is better than I remembered. How can they *not* see?"

This unmistakable intimation of hitherto unsuspected treasure was at last sufficient to awaken my interest, and I resolved to sift the matter of *Orpheus* to its bottom. Since I was reluctant to trouble Mr. Barfield with vague suspicions, and since the circumstances of my discovery appealed even more powerfully to my extracurricular interest in detective fiction than to my professional instincts, I postponed an immediate appeal to the author. In the true fashion of fictional detectives in quest of Orphic mysteries, I set out by indirections to find directions out, or at least to discover as much as I could on my own before appealing to authority. My circumspection was abundantly rewarded the next day as I was exploring Barfield's correspondence with Sir George Rostrover Hamilton. Following a letter dated 27 December 1948 was a Programme Ticket for the Little Theatre production of *Orpheus*, which had been performed from the twentieth through the twenty-fifth of September. Besides Lewis's "blurb" (slightly emended), it contains Barfield's original commentary on the play, which is reprinted (slightly emended) in the present volume.

Lest I should be thought singularly obtuse, I should perhaps observe at this point that I did inquire whether the Bodleian had a copy of the play. Lewis's blurb had in fact been quite sufficient to prompt such an inquiry, especially in the light of its Wheatonian context. But the arrangement with Wheaton College which provided for the duplication of Lewis's materials did not extend in general to Barfield's productions. So I was forced to fall back on more direct methods. The loss of aesthetic detachment was, however, more than compensated by the revelation which ensued.

Feeling that I now had sufficient evidence to warrant an accusation—What's all this about a play? Why was I not told?—I called Barfield on the telephone and confronted him with my facts. He immediately confessed to having written such a play, and under further questioning he admitted that he might have a copy lying about somewhere in his study. ("Confessed" is of course an hyperbole, a license inspired by the metaphor of detective fiction, but it is only a slight exaggeration of Barfield's initial reluctance to have the whole question of *Orpheus* brought to light again.) When I asked him if I might see it, he graciously consented, and though it was his only copy, he even went so far as to allow me to carry it back with me to this country. Though I was somewhat reassured by the existence of that other copy in Wheaton, I literally did not allow the typescript out of my sight.

My first reading of the play, on the plane back to the States, struck me with the force of a revelation; though I was more or less prepared for an exceptional insight into Barfield's genius, nothing that he or Lewis had said about the play quite prepared me for the immediate experience of it, or for the shock of recognition: here is the evolution of consciousness made flesh, the thing itself in human form, the myth made fact as imaginative experience. As I began to digest this experience, I felt almost at once that the play should be—must be—published. When I reread the play, in somewhat more leisurely fashion, my first impulse grew into a settled conviction: if Barfield himself were reluctant to pursue the matter, I would seek to do so myself and to make whatever practical arrangements were necessary. And so it fell out. When I first raised the question with him, he expressed "an invincible repugnance to pushing that or any other verse" of his. Fortunately, his repugnance did not extend to my attempting to have *Orpheus* published: "Naturally I should be glad all the same to see it in print, and if you really feel the inclination, time and energy to have a shot, well . . . more power to your elbow!"

Granted this license, I resolved to become a sort of Orphic midwife, *et redactor et bucinator Orpheos*, and so began to shape myself by degrees into a species of editor *cum* literary agent. The editorial and critical parts of my enterprise—correcting the typescript and writing about the play—were an unalloyed delight. I even prided myself that I had occasionally helped the author to clarify his intention. The sustained attention which I was compelled to give to the details of the text served only to nourish, and was itself nourished by, my attempt to form a coherent critical assessment of the whole. As *Orpheus* became more and more a part of my own imaginative life, and I began to feel that I was in some measure participating in its recreation, I was often led to recall Lewis's pithy observation: "It is better than I remembered." And Barfield's response to all of this was even more deeply gratifying. Besides flattering me with the suggestion that I had more than once penetrated to the true mystery of the play, he expressed very powerfully his own quickening interest in bringing *Orpheus* once more to light: "Your letter," he wrote at one point, has "agitated me! *Orpheus* is not used to being taken so earnestly. What he *is* used to is being forgotten all about. Result: there is a kind of Rip van Winkle resuscitation of an old Barfield of the late '30s going on, which is of course not unpleasurable, but is certainly agitating."

The rest of the story is now more or less a matter of historical record: you hold the result in your hand. And there my tale of fortune would have its natural ending, but for the fact that I have incurred further debts of gratitude which I am delighted to acknowledge. My greatest debt is to Professor Thomas Kranidas, for his encouragement and for bringing *Orpheus* to the attention of the Lindisfarne Press. As plans for publication were being brought into shape, I found it necessary to revise my own commentary, to bring it up to date, to clarify some of its accidental obscurities, and to flesh out some of the sketchier connections I had tried to draw between *Orpheus* and Barfield's other work. In this research I was greatly assisted, materially by a Humanities Grant from the University of Arizona, and spiritually by the wisdom of Professor Georg Tennyson and the generous enthusiasm of Professor Jane Hipolito. In point of fact, Professor Hipolito's assistance was also material, since she allowed me to peruse, and to plunder, her extensive bibliography of Barfield's work.

Finally, having sought to thank those whose kindness and generosity have assisted and encouraged my own efforts, and to acknowledge the active industry of those who have made this celebration possible, I have still to thank the founder of the feast. Perhaps the most useful way to express my gratitude to Mr. Barfield for having created *Orpheus* is to reflect briefly on the nature of his achievement, and to measure the peculiar, poetic excellence of *Orpheus* against the general quality of his other published writings.

Inasmuch as it reflects a similar depth of imaginative insight, the *Orpheus* is clearly of a piece with all of Barfield's other major work; its essence is the rediscovery, the recreation, of meaning. What G. B. Tennyson has recently said of *History, Guilt and Habit* (1979) is no less true of *Orpheus*: "It is meaning that Barfield gives back to us in the face of all the contemporary assertions that meaning has fled forever." At the same time, however, *Orpheus* possesses an immediacy of imaginative appeal which renders it unique; its meaning is not so much achieved by the reader as given in his immediate experience. More than any of Barfield's other published work, *Orpheus* is fully mythopoeic, not because it is about a myth, but because it is the imaginative recreation of myth itself as an immediate experience. Though the play has been shaped by, and is in some sense the expression of, Barfield's ideas about myth, it is not *about* those ideas. It is, rather, a poetic reincarnation of myth itself, a concrete embodiment of the poet's imaginative life discovered in the myth. And for this reason, the play is easier to grasp, as an experience, than Barfield's other work.

With the exception of certain relatively minor efforts, like *The Silver Trumpet* (1925) and *This Ever Diverse Pair* (1950), the great majority of Barfield's published work is characterized by a certain argumentative density. Even a relatively popular work like *History in English Words* (1925) makes an unremitting demand on the reader's imaginative participation. And it is this quality, I think, which makes his work seem difficult: his basic assumptions must be actively grasped rather than merely acquiesced in. Once one has got hold of his argument, it is easy enough to follow; in the graceful medium of Barfield's style, even the most complex ideas become lucid, without losing any of their evocative subtlety. Indeed, the argument becomes progenitive: one finds oneself anticipating the sort of development that will come next. But getting hold of the argument may be another matter altogether. Barfield's conception of mind, and of the subject-object relation *within* the mind, is radically at odds with some of our most widely held assumptions about the nature of things. Moreover, his ultimate appeal is not to the understanding or the senses but to imagination and reason; we are called upon again and again to produce in ourselves that very act of imagination which is the principal subject of investigation.

That crucial act of imagination is both the method and the aim of all Barfield's work. As he cheerfully proclaims in his introduction to *The Rediscovery of Meaning* (1977), he is "always really saying the same thing over and over again." And as he goes on to emphasize, "the 'same thing' that is always being reaffirmed is the importance of penetrating to the antecedent unity underlying apparent or actual fragmentation" (p. 3). Another name for that "antecedent unity" is *polarity*, grasped as an immediate fact of imaginative experience. And polarity, Barfield teaches us, is not a mere duality of opposite quantities, a Cartesian abstraction of mind from matter; it is rather the concrete interpenetration of contrary qualities, as a subject become its own object in the act of self-discovery. And that self-discovery is what Barfield means by the evolution of consciousness. When we experience in ourselves the polar transformation of unconscious inspiration into conscious imagination, we begin to grasp the historical evolution of consciousness as a growth of potential into actual meaning. Thus, as it were by degrees, the experience which Barfield describes in *Poetic Diction* (1928) as a "felt change of consciousness" (p. 48) is transformed into the active imagination of polarity, and that imagination leads him to evolve his seminal insight into evolution itself as a metamorphosis of potential into actual form.

This two-fold emphasis on polarity and the evolution of consciousness can be discerned in Barfield's writings almost from the first. In the unpublished correspondence with C. S. Lewis, which Lionel Adey explores in his monograph on the *Great War*, we observe Barfield's repeated attempts to ascertain the polar relation between subject and object, to perceive them as mutually interdependent parts evolved from an organic whole. At the same time we can begin to glimpse the way this organic polarity expresses itself, historically, as an evolution of unconscious into conscious meaning. This semantic evolution is the primary concern of *History in English Words*; as Professor Tennyson observes, its argument is grounded in "the peculiarly Barfieldian insight amounting to a discovery that the history of language contains within it a record of the evolution of human consciousness." Underlying this historical process, of course, is the polarity of language itself, the metaphoric tension between image and idea. And that is the primary subject of *Poetic Diction*, which "claims to present, not merely a theory of poetic diction, but a theory of poetry: and not merely a theory of poetry, but a theory of knowledge" (p. 14). Among the many insights afforded by Barfield 's argument is the crucial perception that mental activities which we ordinarily take to be discrete, as prosaic analysis and poetic synthesis, are in fact interdependent, and that it is only through their interpenetration that we are able to construct the "real world" of our objective experience. So it is that genuine knowledge, as distinct from superficial understanding, always requires the participation of the knower in the known.

Participation is, of course, the central idea of *Saving the Appearances* (1957). Where the primary theme of *Poetic Diction* is the capacity of imagination to recreate the past in the present moment of aesthetic awareness, as a polarity between the meaning "given" in language itself and its present metaphoric extension into new meaning, *Saving the Appearances* takes our awareness of history itself as its principal subject; it explores the power of language "to mediate transition from the unindividualized, dreaming spirit that carried the infancy of the world to the individualized human spirit, which has the future in its charge" (*Poetic Diction*, p. 23). And it is this sense of the present as a polarity of past and future which gives Barfield's historical study of Coleridge its peculiar relevance to our own epistemological concerns. For Barfield's description of Coleridge's thinking is also an apt description of *What Coleridge Thought* (1971): it is itself a "radical critique of one or two major presuppositions, upon which the immediate thinking, and as a result the whole cultural and social structure of this 'epoch of the understanding and the senses' (including supposedly radical revolts against it) is so firmly—or is it now infirmly?—established" (p. 11).

Broadly speaking, Barfield's other books can be thought of as so many attempts to suggest the relevance of his ideas to the cultural and social issues of modern life, to remind us again and again that our consciousness has evolved out of earlier forms of awareness, and to insist that the tension between external nature and our inward experience of it, a tension which we commonly experience as an alienating dichotomy of matter and mind, is in fact a polarity, recoverable in conscious experience as an interpenetration of object and subject. The essays in *Romanticism Comes of Age* (1944; enlarged 1966) elaborate one of the central propositions underlying the collective argument of

History in English Words, Poetic Diction, and *Saving the Appearances*: that the Romantics first sought to do consciously what primitive man had done unconsciously, to participate in their phenomena. A mature Romantic outlook, grounded especially in what Coleridge thought, seeks to unite "modern symbol and ancient myth, imagination and inspiration in a single structure firmly bedded in the dimension of history, to show that, when so united, they may become an instrument for the kind of action required to be taken in our present predicament" (p. 21). *Worlds Apart* (1963) speaks directly to that predicament. Seeking to break down the "watertight compartments" which characterize so much modern thought, it employs Socratic dialogue as a means to heal our fragmented consciousness. Evolving through mere dualities of conflicting viewpoints, the dialogue struggles toward a polar interpenetration of ideas, and so toward the central Barfieldian affirmation that imaginative participation "through the symbol in the symbolized" (p. 207) is the ground of human consciousness: "Thinking," as the anthroposophist Sanderson says, "becomes conscious in me to the extent that I make it my act" (p. 174). And this act is the starting point for *Unancestral Voice* (1965). The essential polarity of consciousness is first aphorized—"interior is anterior"—and then developed into a vision of evolution as a spiritual process actively wrought by a "transforming agent." As in *Saving the Appearances*, the Incarnation is contemplated as the central moment in human history: the antecedent Unity of unities, "the uncreated light, the untransformed transforming, entered [the human] consciousness [of Jesus] and became also the Christ of history" (p. 113).

If this crucial moment of realized consciousness suggests a movement of imagination toward mystical vision, the remaining books polarize this tendency by applying mystical insight to issues more immediately practical, more obviously relevant to the dilemmas of modern secular life. *Speaker's Meaning* (1967) explores the polar relation between expression and communication in order to disclose the evolved, "constricted" consciousness of modern man and to suggest present uses of the creative imagination to expand our awareness once again, to recover, by recreating, the meaning that is given in language itself. *The Rediscovery of Meaning and Other Essays* explores various directions—spiritual, aesthetic, scientific, social—in which our awareness might be expanded. In the various matters of which it treats—psychology, philosophy, and religion—Barfield's imagination seeks always to penetrate to that "interior unity informing the *disjecta membra*" (p. 7) of our mental, psychic, and social experience, and to ground itself in "the concrete realities of nature and human nature" (p. 215). And *History, Guilt and Habit* is even more insistently relevant in its central insight, that our responsibility for our own evolution, and for the evolution of all Nature, "will only be discharged, if at all, not by tinkering with the outside of the world but by changing it, slowly enough no doubt, from the inside" (p. 92).

Freedom, responsibility, the transformation of unconscious impulse into conscious volition—these themes, as they are focused by the idea of polarity and directed toward the evolution of our consciousness, suggest the pervasive relevance of Barfield's prophetic insight into the crucial issues of our time. If we will know the truth, he argues, and only if we participate actively in our knowing, as makers rather than mere spectators, we shall be able to liberate ourselves from the prison of ignorance and self-deception. That is relevance with a vengeance—more reality, perhaps, than mankind can easily bear. Barfield's crucial significance, however, is not to be defined by the timeliness with which he addresses specific issues of current concern—isolation, alienation, and consequent guilt, or the dehumanization of man by technological abstraction and our possibly consequent reduction to atomic dust. In many of these areas, indeed, Barfield has anticipated our current crises, as prophets are wont to do. As the *Orpheus* makes clear, for example, he foresaw the actual, radical evil of totalitarianism before it was made flesh in Nazi Germany. Long before Creationism became fodder for our journalistic cannons, Barfield was pointing out the radical inconsistencies in the popular, Darwinian view of evolution. He has indeed been reading the signs of our times, and he may have helped to create, as well as to foresee, some of our present dissatisfactions with positivistic ways of thinking. But this way of signifying his relevance is suggestive rather than definitive. The root of the whole matter, as Barfield has repeatedly said, is his attempt to develop in himself, and to encourage in his readers, that genial power of imagination which alone enables consciousness to penetrate our experience of the world and ourselves in order to reach what lies behind it, to discover the meaning of our existence. For this purpose, the participation of mankind in its own creation, only a truly liberated imagination will serve, an imagination at once deeply in tune with its origins, in the life of nature, and at the same time fully conscious of its individual responsibility for recreating nature. And as Barfield said in *Saving the Appearances*, "it is of the very nature of imagination that it cannot be *inculcated*. There must be first of all the voluntary stirring from within. It must be, not indeed self-created, but certainly self-willed" (p. 179). And for imagination to be willed effectively, it must be awakened, so that it becomes a fully conscious activity.

The great advantage of *Orpheus*, from this point of view, is that it does not immediately require any such *conscious* effort. Imagination cannot be inculcated, but it can be, in some measure, *inspired* by aesthetic experience. The "felt change of consciousness" which Barfield explores in *Poetic Diction* is inherently progenitive: it can reproduce itself in our imagination, as if by a kind of unconscious imitation, and as an immediate experience rather than as a reflection upon that experience. And so it is with *Orpheus*: simply as an imagined experience it embodies, in Coleridge's phrase, "the mind's self-experience in the act of thinking," not reflectively, as an argument about, but immediately, as the experience of a subject which is its own object. *Orpheus* is not an exposition of Barfield's ideas but a concrete embodiment of his thinking, in which the reader's participation is implicit.

To assist that participation, however, it may be useful to recall the substance of Barfield's thinking about the nature of consciousness. A brief recapitulation of *Saving the Appearances* is perhaps the best way to achieve that end, for it is both the most comprehensive development of Barfield's ideas and their most concise expression. For our present purpose it has the further advantage that its argument is most nearly analogous to the action of *Orpheus*. For just as *Orpheus* progresses from unconscious, dreaming awareness to full waking consciousness, so *Saving the Appearances* is an "outline sketch . . . for a history of human consciousness" (p. 13). Barfield traces the evolution of consciousness, and its corollary, the evolution of phenomena, from what he calls "original participation," through "nonparticipating," objective thought, to the possibility of "final participation." In original participation man experiences phenomena as representations of an immaterial other; his relation to appearances is not merely external, through the senses, but internal, through the spirit in which he participates. Objective thinking does not participate in phenomena, does not experience its phenomena as representative of anything; the only conscious relation that the mind has with objects is through the senses. Final participation re-establishes an extra-sensory relation between the mind and phenomena; appearances are self-consciously perceived as representations of man himself, of the spirit dwelling *within* him (rather than, as in original participation, on the other side of the phenomena).

The argument of *Saving the Appearances* begins by examining participation generally and original participation in particular. If we reflect on the activity of perception, we discover that anything presented to consciousness as an object is in fact a *representation*, the product of an interaction between a formless other—the "given" of physical science—and our sensations. The transformation of an undefined "given" into a representation is dependent on some sort of mental activity. In order to experience anything *as* something, an act of construction "is required in us to convert sensations into 'things' "; this activity Barfield calls *figuration* (p. 24). Since we are not ordinarily conscious of our figuration, we do not experience objects as representative of anything; when the activity of representation is thus unconscious, it is useful to refer to the products of figuration simply as appearances, or *phenomena*. Any phenomenon may be perceived as a representation, but it may also be perceived simply as an "object," and that is how we ordinarily perceive it. We must bear in mind, however, that all our common experience of phenomenal nature is produced, collectively, by our figuration; the whole world of familiar nature is in fact a system of "collective representations" (p. 20).

Now, what Barfield calls "original participation" is characterized precisely by the *conscious* experience of phenomena *as* representations of some "other" standing behind them. A tree, for example, was not simply, or even primarily, an object in space; it was a "stopping place" for "Mana," a manifestation of spirit. Primitive man was "not detached, as we are, from the representations." Whereas "the only connection *of which we are conscious* is the external one though the senses" (p. 31), he was conscious also of an *internal*, supersensible connection with the life-principle, which was manifested in the phenomena. This consciousness depended not merely on a different conception but on a different figuration from ours. In original participation, that which is represented is experienced as outside of man, on the other side of the representations. On the other hand, "if our participation, having been first understood and accepted . . . as a fact, should then become a conscious experience, it would have to take the form of a conscious (instead of, as now, unconscious) figuration"; in final participation we would experience the represented within ourselves (p. 41).

Once we moved beyond pre-historic, originally participating awareness, the history of consciousness is primarily a history of the ways in which objective thinking has altered our collective representations by transforming the figuration which produces them. Objective thinking had begun with participated representations, but "the very nature and aim" of pure objective thinking is "to exclude participation" by distinguishing between ourselves as subject and the thing thought about as object (p. 43). We are thus cut off from participation in the phenomena. Our collective representations are based on the supposition that truth is "objective" and sensible rather than supersensibly participated. For a non-participating consciousness, phenomena are dichotomized; an appearance is *either* sensible *or* spiritual, *either* a literal object in space *or* a symbolic representation.

At the same time, however, objective thinking frees phenomena from their nexus in space and time, and by so doing it makes possible the development of memory, and hence of self-consciousness: "When I experience the phenomena in memory, I make them 'mine', not now by virtue of any original participation, but by my own inner activity" (p. 155). And this inner activity may give rise to final participation, which has been made possible in the first place by the loss of original participation. Our ordinary, non-participating consciousness is split between object and subject, "outer and inner . . . thing and thought." But that very disjunction, the polarization of an ancient unity into an outer and an inner meaning, "is the basis of conscious evolution." Meaning was originally experienced, through participation, as *given* in the phenomena themselves, in which meaning was felt to be inherent; now meaning must be *made* and assigned to the phenomena by metaphor, which depends for its existence "precisely on the *absence* of participation" (pp. 121–123). "When we use language metaphorically, we bring it about of our own free will that an appearance means something other than itself, and, usually, that a manifest [outer] 'means' an unmanifest [inner]. We start with an idol [from which participation has been excluded], and we ourselves turn the idol into a representation" (p. 126). When "subconscious organic processes have been sufficiently polarized to give rise to phenomena on the one side and consciousness on the other, memory is made possible. As consciousness develops into self-consciousness, the remembered phenomena become detached or liberated from their originals and so, as images, are in some measure at man's disposal." When the human imagination "chooses to impart to them its own meaning, it is doing, *pro tanto*, with the remembered phenomena what their Creator once did with the phenomena themselves" (pp. 126–127).

Original participation "began as the unconscious identity of man with his Creator"; as man's self-consciousness increased, participation "contracted to a faint awareness of creative activity alike in nature and man, to which was given the name of the Logos or Word." In the Christ original participation was crucified so that it might be reborn as final participation, the *conscious* identity of man with the Creator: "In one man the inwardness of the Divine Name had been fully realized; the final participation, whereby man's Creator speaks from within man himself, had been accomplished. The Word had been made flesh" (p. 170). It is now our part to utter that flesh as Word, consciously and freely: "in original participation, we were dreamers and unfree . . . Christ is a Being who can be participated only in vigilance and freedom" (p. 185).

In Barfield's view, then, the evolution of consciousness implies the fundamental pattern of Christian myth. The evolution of the human spirit "from original to final participation . . . is the progressive incarnation of the Word" (p. 165)—the incarnation, crucifixion, and resurrection of meaning. And this redemptive pattern provides the most conspicuous analogy between the argument of *Saving the Appearances* and the symbolic action of *Orpheus*: the myth of Orpheus, in Barfield's recreation, is a drama of sacrificial death and rebirth.

Eurydice, a Nereid, daughter of the dreaming Sea, is first named and then wedded by Orpheus (the son of Apollo by the Muse Calliope). Orpheus then begins to transform the vague consciousness of Eurydice's original participation into the human self-consciousness which has made him a poet. Eurydice learns to cultivate pleasure for its own sake, by deliberately interrupting her ecstatic experience and repeating it. Her new imaginative freedom, however, leads almost immediately to the death of her consciousness. When she leaves Orpheus, briefly, to enjoy her gift, she is exposed to the lust of Aristaeus (another

son of Apollo by the water nymph Cyrene). Fleeing, she is bitten by a serpent and dies. When she arrives in Hades, she is
asleep, and Hades cannot awaken her.

Desolated by his loss, Orpheus consoles himself with song,
especially through the power that memory has to recreate his
past experience of Eurydice. The beauty of his music is such that
it draws the animals to him and endows them with the power of
speech. In effect, he has projected his self-consciousness back
into nature—as poets of the Romantic movement sought to do.
When the animals beg from him the gift of actual conscious life,
he resolves to sacrifice himself for them by descending to
Hades, in search of Persephone. There he discovers Eurydice
and awakens her. At Persephone's intercession he is allowed to
return with Eurydice to earth—on the condition that he shall
lead the way without once looking back. But Orpheus fails to
complete the sacrifice; he lacks the imaginative faith necessary
to restore Eurydice to life. He fails, Eurydice falls again into the
shades, and Orpheus returns to earth once more alone. Deserted now both by the animals and by the power of music, Orpheus becomes a half-willing sacrifice to the anthropophagous
lust of the Maenads.

Meanwhile, Aristaeus has also suffered a grievous loss; his
bees, which had been both a practical means of livelihood and a
sacred vocation, have perished. Seeking the cause and cure of
his ruin, he visits his mother, Cyrene, who advises him to seek
the help of Proteus, the shape-changer. Acting upon the sea-
god's prophecy, Aristaeus sacrifices a bull to the shade of
Eurydice, whereupon his bees are miraculously restored to him.
"If bees were always bees and nothing more," as Hades had
remarked (II. i), that would be the whole story. But the bees are
messengers, carrying sunlight from the upper air into the lower
regions, breaking down the barrier between the two worlds. As
that barrier finally crumbles, the voices of Orpheus and Eurydice, reunited in Elysium, join the universal chorus as it celebrates the assumption by man of that divinity which died in
nature in order that it might be reborn in the human soul:

> He shall ascend Parnassus awake and find his soul:
> Proteus shall work unsleeping for ever, and forms
> shall flow
> As the meanings of words a poet has mastered. It
> shall be so

That Zeus shall abandon to Cronos the antique
                                    starry crown,
And softly out of Olympus the high gods shall come
                                    down
Shedding ambrosial fragrance in clouds that for ever
                                    abide,
And earth shall be covered with blushes and make
                                    herself sweet as a bride.
And her light shall be liquid as honey, her air taste
                                    good like bread
In the mouths of them that dwell upon earth, and
                                    all shall be fed.

(IV. iii. 110–118)

In spite of its being relatively early, *Orpheus* expresses the ideas even of Barfield's most recent work. And because it is a drama, not an argument, *Orpheus* is of course much more than a statement of ideas; it is, rather, their full imaginative realization. As such, it has much to tell us about the evolution of consciousness and the nature of participation, about imagination and, more generally, the law of polarity.

Insofar as it can be said to be *about* anything, *Orpheus* represents the evolution of human consciousness from its birth in original participation (the dreaming half-consciousness of Nereus, essentially at one with his watery environment), through the growth and death of imagination (reflected by the poetic consciousness of Orpheus, by the growth of Eurydice's self-consciousness and her two-fold death, and by Orpheus's desolation and dismemberment), to the birth of final participation (foreshadowed by the resurrection of Orpheus and Eurydice through the symbolic sacrifice of Aristaeus).

Even more than with the evolution of consciousness, the play has to do with the nature of participation itself, not so much because it is *about* participation as because it *is* a symbol to be participated in. The nature of such symbolism is perhaps shown most explicitly in the second act. Orpheus's participation in Nature has contracted to his consciousness of Nature embodied in Eurydice, his own soul; having lost that soul, he struggles to project his consciousness back *into* Nature, whose voice, now his voice, is articulated by the animals. Orpheus had earlier recollected Eurydice in a kind of tranquility:

> She filled with light the light
> But filled more full the night.
>
> (II. ii. 13–14)

The Swan now re-embodies that memory—"I fill with light the light" (112)—and at the same time makes explicit its idolatrous narcissism:

> But always cruel night
> Shoots from my frowning forehead looped to kiss
> Itself in the clear water.
>
> (113–115)

The animals, who thus take on as their own life the life which Orpheus has given them, are the creation of his poetic imagination.

The argument of the play as a whole is much taken up with matters of poetic activity, in its relation to (original) inspiration on the one hand and (final) creative imagination on the other. Orpheus first implores the inspiration of Mnemosyne to give Eurydice a name and then almost immediately begins to create her consciousness in the image of his own. In the terms suggested by *Poetic Diction*, the Nereids represent 'pure poetry', or rather the unmingled activity of the poetic principle; its contrary, the prosaic principle is represented by Hades and by the absolute, abstract objectivity of his kingdom. At these extremes, however, the polar relation in which synthesis and analysis must subsist has become disjunct: the consciousness of the nymphs is not poetic, cannot even express itself, for it is simply undifferentiated; the wholly dissociated objectivity of Hades results, paradoxically, in an absolute unity of disintegration, where "rightly to be one is, not to be" (II. i. 187). In neither case does imagination operate, destroying in order to recreate; in neither case is the unity *organic*—dependent, that is, upon a consciousness at once fully distinguished and fully unified, in which each part contains the whole. The true, organic polarity of imagination is to be found only in the interpenetration of poetic and prosaic principles, as that is represented in the poetry of Orpheus, and even more in the imaginative relation between Orpheus and Eurydice, in the creative love that suffers death in order to be reborn.

Taken as a whole, the play represents not merely the creative imagination but the universal law of polarity. In Coleridge's words, "Every power in nature and in spirit must evolve an opposite as the sole means and condition of its manifestation: and all opposition is a tendency to reunion." Mind and nature, subject and object, are thus "two forces of a single power," one tending "to expand infinitely," the other seeking "to apprehend or *find* itself in this infinity." The action of Barfield's play expresses the fundamental contrariety—the unity in multeity—of existence as it is grasped by consciousness. Existence manifests itself through the contrariety of life and death, Dionysus and Hades: in seasonal nature as the rhythm of summer and winter, Persephone above and below, in animate nature as the alternation of waking and sleeping—as Eurydice is awakened out of her unconsciousness, returned again to sleep, then again to death, and finally reawakened. Consciousness seeks to grasp its own existence by the power of imagination, destroying in order to recreate, as happens to Orpheus, as had happened to Dionysus, torn apart by the Titans and regenerated by Zeus. And since every polar opposition is the manifestation of a single power, each set of contraries is contained by a third term: Zeus restores life to Dionysus, as Aristaeus does to Orpheus; Demeter redeems Persephone from the underworld, as Persephone redeems Eurydice. In every case, as in every true metaphor, the reconciliation of opposites produces not merely a recovery but a recreation of meaning.

All of this is more or less what one would expect: Barfield's expository writings can provide very useful guides for interpreting his dramatic fiction. Although *Orpheus* is fully perspicuous in its own right, it is nonetheless richly illuminated by the radiance of Barfield's other work. Conversely, the play can be used, not only to illustrate or substantiate, but to elucidate some of Barfield's ideas. What he says, for example, in *Saving the Appearances* about the function of memory in liberating images from original participation is considerably amplified and clarified (as well, of course, as demonstrated) by the argument of the play. Orpheus, the grandson of Memory, explains that repetition, which is the basis of memory, is the fundamental principle of human consciousness:

> He who says: Lo, what I gaze on
> Is the same as even now,
> He abides and knows and loves it
> Clinging: steadfastness is all.

> (I. ii. 72–75)

At the same time that repetition makes consciousness possible, however, it is inherently the enemy of life, and ultimately of consciousness itself, for it is the principle of mechanism. And mechanism is pre-eminently the principle of Hades, where the rule of action is senseless, abstract repetition, empty of life, and even of memory itself. As Barfield observes in his Program Note, Hades is "the region where the principle of lifeless repetition has triumphed, where Sisyphus's stone rolls back to him with the regularity of clockwork." In Sisyphus, who has lost all memory of his former self, and even more strikingly in Tantalus, who has been reduced to pure subjectivity, we see projected and crystalized that life-denying impulse toward the repetitive manipulation of experience which is the death of consciousness as well as life. Held in proper balance, however, with the formless life principle, memory is the basis of living form, which contains life without destroying it—or at least destroys in order to recreate; memory makes possible the transformation of prophetic inspiration (in which the whole of Nature breathes through human life) into creative imagination (by which human consciousness contains Nature). And as the argument of the play demonstrates not merely the ambivalence but the fundamental *polarity* of memory, so the imaginative life of the play manifests the ability of memory, not merely to recall, but actually to *recreate* the past in the present, as Orpheus comes alive in the mind of the audience, the myth reborn.

That coming alive is, of course, the very essence of the drama. To have said even as much as I have about exposition and argument is, perhaps, to have said too much, since it could lead to a mistaken impression both of the play itself and of its most important relation to Barfield's other work. For in no sense should the play be regarded as a mere aggregate of themes, as though the author had set out to put some of his ideas into the play, regarded for this purpose as a persuasive vehicle. (The reader might well find the play persuasive, but that is quite another matter.) The attempt to define themes might in itself suggest that their interrelation is quantitative or merely objective—as if idea *A* in *Saving the Appearances* corresponded to idea *a* in *Orpheus*. In fact, however, the relation is qualitative and organic: the Idea manifests itself now in one now in another form. The true interrelationship is metaphoric: just as every part of *Orpheus*, every theme and image, implies the whole, so *Orpheus* as a whole contains and is contained by the argument of

Barfield's work. For the purpose of interpretation, the coincidence of certain ideas is not nearly so important as the form of the play (the way in which it *actualizes* ideas) and what might be called its texture—the interpenetration of idea and image, sound and sense. It is here that the relations between *Orpheus* and Barfield's other work are most intimate, in the imaginative realm where we participate in the process of thinking itself rather than merely contemplate the products of thought. That qualitative process can perhaps best be suggested by an illustrative instance—a part implying the whole. When he attempts to illuminate the nature of "true poetic metaphor" (the metaphor which reaches beyond mere fanciful association to reveal truth), Barfield often speaks in metaphor: "the world, like Dionysus, is torn to pieces by pure intellect; but the poet is Zeus: he has swallowed the heart of the world; and he can reproduce it as a living body" (*Poetic Diction*, p. 88). At the same time that it expresses the interpenetration of meaning and myth, this metaphor also embodies the very principle of meaning which it seeks to illuminate. In other words, although it contains within itself the principle of its own explanation, the metaphor does not "explain"; it *is* the meaning to be apprehended by the active imagination. That meaning cannot be inculcated; it will never disclose itself to a passive understanding. The reader must actually participate in making the author's meaning, recreating the argument in himself.

The whole of *Orpheus* is metaphoric in precisely that sense; it is a symbol. And as Barfield has more than once pointed out, "it is only when you attend to [a symbol] wholeheartedly instead of speculating on what is behind it . . . that you really reach what is behind it" (*Worlds Apart*, p. 146). A symbol must be participated in. To say of what *Orpheus* is the symbol might partially describe but would inevitably distort its imaginative reality. One might say that the play expresses the growth of a mind becoming fully conscious of itself, with all that such growth must be taken to imply. At one point I asked the author whether it would be appropriate to describe *Orpheus* as a myth of the evolution of consciousness. I was properly answered: "Can you imagine me producing a myth of *anything else*?" And of course I could not; there can be no question of preferring some other meaning. Nonetheless, one could certainly conceive of the play (not adequately but still appropriately) as a myth of sacrificial death and rebirth. Neither meaning, thus defined, either includes or excludes the other; the myth contains both. The meaning of *Orpheus* is limited, not by any discursive framework, but by the degree to which the reader participates, in its making, so that its life becomes his. The life of *Orpheus* is Protean; it will assume almost any shape that is imposed upon it – though of course it will yield up its deepest secrets only in its proper shape. When I reflect on the form which my own participation has most consistently assumed, the shape – the countenance – which it presents to me is myth, or rather the mythopoeic process. The meaning, and making, of myth is a crucial point in Barfield's interpretation of human consciousness; indeed, one might formerly have wished that he had had a good deal more to say directly on the question. Now we have the whole matter of Greek myth (and many of its relations with Hebrew myth) sifted to the bottom, concocted, digested, and finally transformed. What Barfield says in *Poetic Diction* about the nature of mythic consciousness gives only a hint of what is here, in effect, a fully evolved theory of myth – presented, however, not as a set of propositions about mythology, but as the embodiment of mythic consciousness in dramatic form. In *Orpheus* we see revealed the process by which myth becomes conscious and, by becoming conscious of *itself*, reincarnates itself as living meaning, so that what was first spoken by the gods is now uttered by man. And in this way the play becomes a kind of anatomy of Greek myth. By analyzing in order to re-unify, the play transforms the corpus of Greek myth into a new organism; *Orpheus* makes actual the interrelations between various myths which had been hitherto only potential. Thus, for example, the stories of Heracles, of Aristaeus, and of Orpheus are drawn into a single action: as Heracles had extorted the secret of the Hesperides from the shape-changer, Nereus, so Aristaeus compels Proteus to reveal the secret of his own lost paradise; as Heracles had plundered Hell, so Orpheus attempts to regain his lost Eurydice, and as he had gone below to implore the aid of Persephone and her great mother, so Aristaeus must descend to the underwater world where his mother, Cyrene, dwells. Ultimately, the story of Orpheus and Eurydice is also the myth of Demeter and Persephone, wherein "the ideas of waking and sleeping, of summer and winter, of life and death, of mortality and immortality are all lost in one pervasive meaning" (*Poetic Diction*, p. 91). In *Orpheus*, however, which is not myth simply, but myth re-making, that pervasive meaning is *consciously* expressed, not as dream but as poetry. What was lost in unity originally, and subsequently lost in disintegration, has been recreated from within, so that the myth becomes conscious of itself *within* us.

Anyone who has experienced the play, however, will not need to be told that it celebrates the mythopoeic imagination. The appeal of *Orpheus* is, as it was meant to be, immediately symbolic: it is the *sense* of the action, not the critical significance of its themes, which communicates the life of the play. To some readers *Orpheus* will represent an initiation into Barfield's thinking; for them I hope I may have made slightly easier, not the play itself, but the passage from the play to other regions of Barfield's thought. To other readers Barfield's work will already be more or less familiar; in them I hope I may occasionally have awakened a sense of something they might otherwise have missed. Even if I should have failed of these aims, I might still hope to have offered a small tribute to one whose work has made mine possible. In dedicating *The Allegory of Love* to him, C. S. Lewis called Owen Barfield the wisest and best of his unofficial teachers. Readers of *Orpheus* will surely number themselves among those who gladly echo Lewis's sentiment.

JOHN C. ULREICH, JR.
The University of Arizona
Tucson, Arizona

John Ulreich is an Associate Professor of English Literature at the University of Arizona, where he teaches courses in the English Renaissance (chiefly Milton and Spenser), the literature of the Bible, and modern fantasy. In addition to reviews of Barfieldiana — *What Coleridge Thought*, R. J. Reilly's *Romantic Religion*, and Lionel Adey's *C. S. Lewis's "Great War" with Owen Barfield* — he has published articles on Milton, Spenser, Sir Philip Sidney, C. S. Lewis, and the Old Testament. Foremost among his current projects is an authorized biography of Owen Barfield.

Glossary and Guide to Pronunciation

A BRIEF MYTHOLOGICAL GUIDE
to Characters Appearing in,
and Persons and Places
Mentioned in
ORPHEUS

CHARACTERS

Arethusa (ă-rĕ-thū'-să), a wood nymph who, to escape pursuit by the river god Alpheus, was changed by Artemis into an underground stream.

Aristaeus (ă-rĭs-tee'-ŭs), son of Apollo and Cyrene, father of Actaeon, and half-brother of Orpheus.

Ascalaphus (ăs-kăl'-ă-fŭs), Hades' spy, transformed by Persephone into an owl.

Charon (kair'-ŏn), the boatman who ferried the souls of the dead to the underworld.

Cyrene (sī-ree'-nee), a water-nymph beloved by Apollo, to whom she bore Aristaeus.

Danaïds (dăn'-ay-ĭdz), the fifty daughters of Danaus, who commanded them to slay their husbands; only one refused.

Eurydice (eūr-ĭd'-ĭ-see), daughter of Nereus and wife of Orpheus.

Hades (hay'-deez), god of the underworld (also called Hades), ravisher and then husband of Persephone; brother of Zeus and Poseidon.

Maenads (mee'-nădz), female worshipers of Dionysus.

Nereids (nee'-rĭdz), the fifty daughters of Nereus.

Nereus (neer'-eūs), a sea deity, forerunner of Poseidon.

Orpheus (orf'-eūs), son of Apollo and Calliope.

Persephone (per-sĕf'-ŏ-nee), daughter of Demeter, and Hades' Queen; she spends half the year (summer) with her mother, the other half (winter) with her husband.

Satyr(s) (say'-tŭr), nature spirits, half man and half goat; followers of Dionysus and companions of Pan.

Sisyphus (sĭs'-ĭ-fŭs), for attempting to cheat death, is punished by having to roll a huge rock up a cliff, only to have it roll down again as he reaches the top.

Tantalus (tan'-tă-lŭs), for having fed his son, Pelops, to the gods, is tormented by being unable to drink from the river in which he stands or to eat from the cluster of grapes above his head.

MENTIONED

Acheron (ăk'-ĕr-ŏn), Sorrow, one of the rivers of Hades.

Actaeon (ak-tee'-ŏn), the son of Aristaeus, was turned into a stag by Artemis (Chastity) and killed by his own hounds.

Aegean (ee-jee'-ăn), the sea between Greece and Asia Minor, named after Aegeus, the father of Theseus.

Aphrodite (af-rō-dī'-tee), goddess of generation and human love.

Apollo (ă-pŏl'-ō), the Sun God, father of Orpheus and Aristaeus.

Argus (ăr'-gŭs), a creature with a hundred eyes, set by Hera to guard Io, beloved of Zeus; slain by Hermes.

Artemis (ăr'-tĕ-mĭs), twin sister of Apollo, virgin goddess of the Moon, chastity and hunting.

Avernus (ă-vĕr'-nŭs), an entrance to Hades; also one of the rivers of the underworld.

Beroë (bĕr'-ō-ee), one of the Oceanides (sea nymphs), attendant upon Cyrene.

Cadmus (kăd'-mŭs), founder of Thebes and father of Semele.

Calliope (kă-lī'-ŏ-pee), daughter of Zeus and Mnemosyne, Muse of heroic poetry; mother of Orpheus.

Cerberus (sŭr'-bŭr-ŭs), the three-headed dog of the underworld.

Cronos (kro'-nŏs), a Titan whose union with Rhea produced Zeus, Poseidon, and Hades, who eventually overthrew their father and placed Zeus on the throne of heaven. The reign of Cronos had been associated with a Golden Age on earth.

Clymene (klĭm'-ĕ-nee), a Nereid, attendant upon Cyrene.

Clytaemnestra (klī-tĕm-nĕs'-tră), daughter of Leda and Zeus, who came to Leda in the form of a swan; twin sister of Helen and wife of Agamemnon, whom she slew to avenge his sacrifice of their daughter, Iphigenia.

Cocytus (kō-kī'-tŭs), Lamentation, one of the rivers of Hades.

Deïopeia (dee-ĭ-o-pee'-ă), a Nereid, attendant upon Cyrene.

Demeter (dee-mee'-tĕr), The Earth-Mother goddess, mother of Persephone.

Dionysus (dī-ŏ-nice′-us), the Wine-God, son of Zeus and Semele, or Persephone (to whom Zeus presented himself in the form of a serpent). When Semele demanded that Zeus appear to her in his proper form, his radiance burned her to a cinder; Zeus preserved the fetal Dionysus in his thigh, whence in due course he was born.

Drymo (drī′-mo), a sea nymph, one of the attendants of Cyrene.

Elysium (ĕ-lĭz′-ĭ-ŭm), the dwelling place reserved for the spirits of the blessed.

Erebus (ĕr′-ĕ-bŭs), the underworld, particularly the region through which the virtuous passed on their way to Elysium.

Evoe (ay′-vō-ay′), the ritual cry of the Maenads.

Giants (jī′-ents), sons of Uranus (Heaven) and Ge (Earth), who sprung from the wound given Uranus by his son Cronos; they were cast into Tartarus when they attempted a rebellion against Zeus.

Helen (hel′-ĕn), daughter of Leda and Zeus, twin sister of Clytaemnestra, wife of Menelaus (brother of Agamemnon); Helen's abduction by Paris caused the Trojan war.

Hephaestus (hĕ-fice′-tŭs), god of fire and metal work, unlovely husband of Aphrodite.

Hera (hee′-ră), daughter of Cronos and Rhea, wife of Zeus.

Herakles (heer′-ă-kleez), the greatest hero of the ancient world. His eleventh labor was stealing the golden apples of the Hesperides, whose secret he had forced Proteus to reveal; his twelfth was bringing the hell-hound Cerberus up to earth.

Hesperides (hes-pĕr′-ĭ-deez), paradisal gardens in the far west, in which there were golden apples guarded by a dragon.

Hesperus (hes′-pĕr-ŭs), the evening star, father of the Hesperides.

Hippocrene (hĭp-o-kree′-nee), a spring on Mount Helicon, sacred to the Muses.

Iacchus (ee-ak′-ŭs), another name of Dionysus.

Lethe (lee′-thē), Oblivion, one of the rivers of Hades.

Marsyas (mar′-sĭ-ăs), a satyr who challenged Apollo to a contest of musical ability.

Metis (meet′-ĭs), an Oceanid. She was the first wife of Zeus, who swallowed her when he learned she was pregnant; Athena was later born out of Zeus′ head.

Minos (mĭn'-ŏs), king of Crete, father of the Minotaur, supreme judge of the underworld.

Mnemosyne (mnee-moz'-i-nee), Memory, the mother of the Muses, who inspire all human arts.

Oceanus (o-see'-a-nus), a Titan, god of the stream surrounding earth.

Olympus (ō-lĭm'-pŭs), sacred mountain of the gods.

Pan (pan), part man, part goat; the god of shepherds.

Peleus (peel'-ēus), married Thetis, a Nereid, by whom he begot Achilles.

Peneus (pee-nee'-ŭs), a river in Thessaly, home of Cyrene.

Phlegethon (flĕg'-ĕ-thŏn), Fire, one of the rivers of Hades.

Philomela (fĭl-ŏ-may'-lă), sister of Procne, raped by her sister's husband, Tereus, and transformed into a nightingale.

Phoebus (fee'-bŭs), Brightness, a name of Apollo.

Phyllodoce (phĭl-lŏd'-o-kee), one of Cyrene's attendant nymphs.

Procne (prōk'-nee), sister of Philomela, wife of Tereus.

Proteus (prō'-tēus), a sea deity, shape-changer, and prophet.

Rhadamanthus (răd-ă-man'-thŭs), of Crete, became a judge of the underworld.

Semele (sĕm'-ĕ-lee), daughter of Cadmus, mother of Dionysus; when Zeus appeared to her in his divine radiance, she was burned to ash, but Zeus preserved their fetal son in his thigh, from which in due course, Dionysus was born.

Styx (stĭx), Hatred, one of the rivers of Hades.

Taenarus (tee'-nă-rŭs), an entrance to the underworld.

Tartarus (tar'-tă-rŭs), the place in the underworld where sinners were punished.

Tempe (tĕm'-pee), a famous valley in Thessaly.

Tereus (tee'-rēus), husband of Procne, ravisher of Philomela.

Theseus (thee'-sēus), slew the Minotaur in the Labyrinth of Crete.

Thetis (thĕ'-tĭs), a Nereid, was the mother of Achilles by Peleus.

Titans (tī'-tănz), offspring of Uranus and Ge (Heaven and Earth), were overthrown by Zeus and other Olympian deities.

Uranus (yoo-ra'-nŭs), Father Sky.

Zeus (zēus), Father of gods and men, especially of Dionysus and Persephone.

Owen Barfield was born in 1898. Well-known today as a philosopher and literary critic, and as a seminal influence in the revival of "romantic religion," he is the author of, among other works, *History in English Words* (1926), *Poetic Diction* (1928), *Romanticism Comes of Age* (1944), *Saving the Appearances* (1957), *Worlds Apart* (1963), *Unancestral Voice* (1965), *What Coleridge Thought* (1971), and *History, Guilt and Habit* (1979).

Owen Barfield, photographed at the Lindisfarne Mountain Retreat in Crestone, Colorado during a conference on *The Evolution of Consciousness*, Summer 1982. Photograph by Judy Van Hook.

ACKNOWLEDGMENTS

The author and publisher wish to thank the following for their help in making this edition possible: Lionel Adey, Christy and Henry Barnes, Peggy Beacom, Donald L. Benson, Mr. and Mrs. J. L. Benson, Michael Colby, The Cultural Freedom Fund of the Tides Foundation, James Cutsinger, John Davy, Joan P. Dufault, Ed Engelmann, Michael Eigen, Peter Elliston, Howard Fulweiler, Manning Goodwin, H. S. Vaughn Henry, William Hunt, Jeanne Hunter, Maulsby Kimball, Hope M. Kirkpatrick, Shirley and Sol Kort, Thomas Kranidas, Robert F. Lehman, Kevin Lewis, Anna Lups, Robert McDermott, John and Virginia Micetich, Clifford Monks, Judith and Joseph Moser, Alastair C. K. Munro, Konrad Oberhuber, Marion Ottery, R. J. Reilly, M. C. Richards, Mrs. Robert H. Richards, Douglas and Fern Sloan, Brian Stockwell, G. B. Tennyson, Bruce and Katherine Weber, The William C. Whitney Foundation, Nancy L. Wood, Arthur Zajonc, Gary Zukav, and many others who chose to remain anonymous.

A Note on the Lindisfarne Press of the Lindisfarne Association

The Lindisfarne Association is an educational and cultural organization preparing the ground for the resacralization of culture. Specifically it upholds, within the natural diversity of a planetary epoch, the following four goals: the transformation of individual consciousness; the understanding of the inner harmony of the world's great religious traditions; the illumination of the spiritual dimensions of world order; and the creation of an ecologically and spiritually appropriate meta-industrial culture. Within this context, the Lindisfarne Press seeks to disseminate and make available materials conducive to such a culture of true values and creative of a new harmony in and between humanity, nature and the divine. Its range therefore includes: anthropology, psychology, politics, economics, biology, theology, philosophy, metaphysics, architecture, ecology, poetry and art. For information on programs and publications, please write: The Lindisfarne Press, R.D. 2, West Stockbridge, Massachusetts 01266, U.S.A.